A Window on Folk Dance

A Window on Folk Dance

with special reference to the
dances of the Iberian Peninsula

BY LUCILE ARMSTRONG
EDITED BY DIKI GLEESON

SPRINGFIELD BOOKS LIMITED

Published by Springfield Books Limited, Norman Road, Denby Dale,
Huddersfield HD8 8TH, West Yorkshire, England.

First edition 1985

Design: Douglas Martin
Illustration: Anne Isseyegh

Typesetting: Paul Hicks Limited, Middleton, Manchester
Printed and bound in England
by Netherwood Dalton & Co, Huddersfield

Armstrong, Lucile
A window on folk dance:
with special reference to the Iberian Peninsula
1. Folk dancing – History
I. Title II. Gleeson, Diki
793.3'1'09 GV1743

ISBN 0-947655-04-2

Dedication

I DEDICATE THIS BOOK firstly to the people of Spain and Portugal. Both peasants and fishermen have taught me so much which was not contained in the available books on folklore. This book is also dedicated to Violet Alford, without whose tuition and patient instruction over very many years I would never have undertaken the study of folk dance, its origins and meaning.

Lucile Armstrong, *London, 1985*

Contents

Acknowledgements

I WISH TO THANK Mrs Patricia Hursey for her devotion in typing out the whole of the first draft of the typescript.

I also wish to thank Mr Charles Steventon for useful suggestions and for writing the Foreword.

And a special thank you to Mrs Diki Gleeson, without whose assistance this work would not have been published, for her untiring efforts in editing and retyping and help in many other ways.

Lucile Armstrong, *London, 1985*

Foreword

Mrs Lucile Armstrong, who is the author of several books on folk dances of the Iberian Peninsula, has spent much of her colourful life travelling and studying folk dances in many parts of the world. She learnt the dances, often in remote villages, and made meticulous notes and sketches to enable her to pass on the dances to groups in London where she became well known as an authority on traditional folk dances. Groups from her classes have given many displays, including several at the Royal Albert Hall. All of these were in the appropriate costumes and were danced to authentic music and song.

Lucile has always been intrigued by the meaning of traditional dances, and the fact that many of these, from different countries, had similar figures and movements. This book records the considerable research carried out by Lucile over many years into the subject. It shows how the dances of the early tribes were closely related to man's survival. The crops to feed the people of the village needed sun and water, and man himself needed the horse to assist in his labours and the bull to provide meat for food. From these necessities grew a whole range of dances to worship the sun, moon, water, fire, horse, bull, to ensure the provision of food and security. Other dances were devised to encourage fertility or to drive away evil spirits. The costumes worn during such dances were also related to the indigenous materials and to the traditions and customs of the tribe.

Lucile describes in detail the relationship of many dance figures and costumes to man's vital need for survival. These individual dances reach a climax in colourful festivals, descriptions of several of which are included.

As an acknowledged authority in the folk dance world, Lucile has also acted as adjudicator for many years at the well-known Llangollen folk festival.

The serious student of folk dance culture will find this book a unique and fascinating record.

Charles Steventon
Chairman, Society for International Folk Dancing
London, 1985

Introduction

'MUDAR COSTUMBRE A PAR DE MUERTE' – to change a custom is as bad as death – is an old Spanish proverb which perhaps overstates the case, but does underline the importance of the repetitive and recognisable bedrock of society. Custom is important. It transmits confidence, allays anxiety, relieves man of the agonising bewilderment of choice and presents a framework of discipline with the accompanying freedom and release simultaneously generated.

Dance has always and quite rightly been accepted as one of the very basic atavistic activities and attributes of man and his society. The paintings in the Lascaux Caves, for example, are estimated to be more than 30,000 years old and represent a very high level of culture and social sophistication, quite capable of creating dance forms.

The range and importance of dance can probably still be demonstrated by the few remaining primitive peoples in the last remaining unexplored corners of the world. In some ways it is robust, a permanently enduring form, but in many other ways it is fragile and ephemeral. Even non-participating observation (particularly in relation to ritual dances), can begin to strike an alteration or change of focus. Leading dancers, especially in dance forms where a leader is prominent, can by their own expertise change, translate and expand the existing forms, sometimes in a damaging way. One has only to move a few villages along in the same area to see the movements and patterns performed to almost identical music or accompaniment, even called by the same name, but nevertheless exhibiting quite a contrast the one with the other.

The uses and reasons for the various dances are legion –

there are dances to gird a hunter's loins, to weave a magic spell for successful hunting, to inspire the participants with courage and energy, to terrify and subdue adversaries or invaders; there are dances recording great deeds to glorify individuals or more likely a group and to keep those powerful conquering vibrations active for that particular clan. That sort of dance is not far from a celebratory victory dance, but then one does often merge or spill into another.

The wealth of dances aimed at ensuring a full harvest from the earth are linked and often identical to those making fertility magic to increase the size and power of the tribe. Some are specific, e.g. rain-making dances (many S.I.F.D. members can vouch for the efficacy of Mayim Mayim!) Others become individual competitive demonstrations, e.g. how high can each dancer leap – the height of the leaps representing the height the crops will achieve later on. Stamping is often a part of this ritual, to awaken the earth in spring to burgeon forth. Then there are all the many varieties of dances derived or inspired by the village/group labour, from woodcutting or blacksmithing to spinning and sewing; sometimes the actual movements are reproduced, sometimes the patterns involved, as with some of the weaving dances where long ribbons are actually woven in the dance and a finished 'cloth' held up at the end, or the weaving dances where the movements and pattern correspond to the movement and paths of the shuttles, beaters, etc., on the loom. Another group of dances can be said to emanate from skill-improving rituals like those that practise for example fan waving, throwing and gesturing as in the East. There are dances of welcome and celebration, dances for special occasions, different seasons, religious festivals and festivities. Movement has always been a universal expression of feeling and endeavour for man. It can always be therapeutic – either incidentally or specifically and there are certainly curative forms, not just the necessity for dancing away the poison of a tarantula. Expiation, relief, satisfaction, renewal: all have their place. As complicated, interesting, challenging, vital and many-faceted as man himself is, so correspondingly are his dances and their endless variety.

Lucile Armstrong has spent a large part of her mercifully quite long life gathering experience, information and understanding of part of this rich, endlessly intriguing wealth that is dance. However much it is mined, there are always rich new seams to be tapped. Her special field of study has been mainly Iberian folk dance and there are many who are well aware of her great expertise in both the singing and dancing of the various regions throughout the Peninsula. All those of us in any way interested in any part of this world heirloom must be grateful that Lucile has now committed some of this knowledge and appreciation to paper, here, in this interesting book so charmingly and simply written. Throughout her life she has 'guarded' authenticity. For many years she has been one of the most respected, indeed revered, adjudicators at the Llangollen Eisteddfod's folk dance, music and song days, which have become known and cherished as a force for maintaining and sustaining authenticity, accuracy of intent, pattern, costume, presentation – all aspects of the dance (and song) offered in this unique international competition. Throughout the folk dancing world Lucile is rightly acknowledged and acclaimed; her book will be well received and long treasured.

Diki Gleeson, *Enfield, 1985*

CHAPTER ONE

The origins

THE NEED FOR AUTHENTICITY

THE AIM of this little book is to remind folk dancers that when they dance, it is not only for the enjoyment of performing (although that is probably the chief reason now) but at the same time to be aware as far as possible of the meanings and origins of the steps and figures and to try to 'tune in' to the feelings and aspirations which created them, because although we have lost so many of the reasons for particular parts of the dance, I feel it is important and a part of a valuable heritage (of the world) that we try to maintain and preserve these dances in their traditional way. They have been handed down as an important heirloom and we are forsaking and abandoning our ancestors if we turn our back on accuracy (as we know it and appreciate it) and try instead to elaborate/improve/adorn their offerings. For example, the original sword dance from Bursa has been spoilt by a leader, not knowing the origins of ritual dance and thinking that sword dance must mean fighting dance, inventing several more 'war-like' figures, thus adulterating what had been a remarkable and imposing dance.

I know that very often a communal, shared, unique and very special feeling and oneness is felt as a group among those people steeped in, for instance, the dancing of the Balkans, where so often dances are a closed or open circle with the dancers being joined by belt, arm or hand and in fairly close contact. With the hypnotic effect of the music and repeated complicated rhythms the dancers almost enter a trance and move as one without consciously making any effort to do so. That is a very marked example of what I think can be expected and hoped for in all folk dancing. And that is the valuable link with its origins. Without conscious understanding there is a link, however tenuous and fragile, with the ancient purposes, needs and beliefs of earlier times.

In this complicated, scientific, harsh world which often seems to us old ones to be getting further and further away from basic life sources, there is a need to feel part of a larger, human, feeling world. Dance breaks down all barriers of language, class and creed; dancers can become united and share a loving spirit through music and the fellowship of such movement. This is a heritage not to be adulterated or tampered with for selfish, temporary reasons, so I plead that you seek to be loyal, faithful and truthful in all your dancing and contacts/influence on dancers and dances.

Throughout history, mighty conquerors have sought to subjugate vanquished peoples through suppressing all that makes those peoples, dance being one of the things that exhibit and show for all to see the unique character of that particular race/tribe. The fact that dance was like a talisman of their core personality is evidenced by, for example, the silent kolos of the Balkans (danced in defiance of their overlords). Secret dancing to the rhythmic whisperings of the dancing feet inspired the young men to fight for their freedom and the restoration of their individuality.

Since many of my pupils have asked for explanations of the figures contained in the folk dances that we performed, I hope the following indications will help them to understand.

It is also my hope that having had the patience to read through this book, readers will be encouraged to learn folk dances – be they of the Iberian Peninsula or elsewhere – with a view to preserving them as the dances were taught, and *not* to make up spectacular demonstrations to astonish the spectators. Since there is always 'a reason why', 'a reason when' and 'a reason where' in folk dance, it is essential that these three reasons should be preserved; they were evolved by our forefathers struggling to solve the everyday problems of their lives, just as we try to do nowadays. How they achieved these aims is reflected in folk dances, so they are very precious material, which we must not alter or 'improve', especially if the object is for our personal glory (which last is, in any case, only very temporary!)

THE BACKGROUND

To understand folk dance properly, it is necessary to know the background thoroughly, and to know the mentality of the people who perform these dances, when they perform them, why the dances are performed and who dances them.

To teach folk dances correctly you must know the meaning of their movements, steps and figures. If you do not know these basic facts you are likely to 'just leave out this bit, alter that part' and so forth, 'to make the dance more attractive, or spectacular'. These remarks I have heard time and time again. Several European countries today have allowed distortions and misconceptions to disfigure their folk dances, all for the sake of making propaganda abroad and trying to show off their dances as more attractive than those of other countries. The perpetrators of this disfigurement are unaware of the irreparable harm they have done to their country and to posterity. Never again will we be able to reconstruct the original dances, because our mentality and our style of living are quite different from those of our ancestors. Traditional folk dances teach us how early man solved his problems. Ancient traditions are an inspiration to us.

The figures or movements and steps meant something vital to their originators. Some were symbols of the psychology of ancient man. Some expressed his beliefs, while some represented the drama of his world and his earnest wish to placate or to invoke his deities and his earnest desire – the desire to live fully.

To understand all this more fully we have great teachers to turn to. The late Professor Carl Jung (*see* Bibliography) was convinced that what was buried in myth and legend is still alive in modern people, even if it only manifests itself through emotional symbols in dreams. Jung discovered that what lies at the very depths of the unconscious bears a strong resemblance to the stages of the spiritual development of man, and what lies buried makes a complete break from the everyday world.

Some of my pupils came to learn the dances just because they yearned for the release of those spiritual forces which lay deep in themselves. Several people have said to me: 'I am not coming to dance any more because I am no longer afraid and I am *sure* of myself.' Ancient folklore had helped the modern psyche.

Another great teacher is Mircea Eliade. He teaches us the fundamental unity upon which folklore in its widest ramifications has been based since neolithic times. In his book *Méphistophélès et l'Androgyne* (p. 267) we read: '. . . psychology has taught us that a symbol delivers its message and fulfils its function even when its significance escapes the conscious mind.' His work is a mine of information and teaches us why we must not alter steps and figures of folk dances handed down to us from our ancestors.

Early man realised that everything in the world had to go through a process of renewal, and tried to assist this process through his dances and songs. He 'washed his soul clean', so to speak, by his shamanistic rites and arts which are found the world over. Some are still performed today.

The march of history cannot be reversed, but we can still learn how early man adjusted to his spiritual evolution and the renewal of his world. By studying his methods we can seek out another way, a modern way of solving our psychological problems. This search is manifest in many ways in our times; in the interest in magic, in shamanistic rites, legends, myths, the occult, in eastern religions. Modern man is trying to come to terms with his fears and anxieties. Primitive man worked out a solution in his own way, for he still could 'walk with the gods' and had access to supernatural powers.

But besides Jung and Eliade we have other teachers: Robert Graves, the poet, for instance, who elucidates so fully meanings hitherto obscure concerning folk customs and beliefs. Others are Sir James Frazer, A.B. Cook, Jane Harrison, E.O. James, E. Mosbacher, J. Marringer, Violet Alford and Gertrude Levy; to mention but a few.* From the point of view of song, we have especially the late Sir Maurice Bowra of Oxford University, with his contribution to the understanding of primitive song, man's use of verse and song as an integral part of his everyday life and to establish these, his connection with the supernatural.

Let us turn to folk dance itself.

Folk dance – not popular dance

Popular dance, mazurkas for instance, was brought into being for society balls and permeated all classes of society. This type of dance becomes the fashion for short periods only.

Folk dances can be ritual, educational, for discipline, therapeutic or community/social, but all were created thousands of years ago, and handed down from generation to generation by tradition. Some ritual dances became social when their ritual purpose was no longer believed in or understood.

WHAT IS FOLK DANCE?

It is an attempt by primitive man to influence supernatural

* Major works are listed in the Bibliography.

forces throughout ritual steps and figures, in order to win favour and help to further human interests. In other words, it is sympathetic magic expressed through movement.

To give a few examples: in some *sword dances* the performers step from side to side, all in a line, to show the Earth Mother how wide the ore seam is to be in the mines, so that man can extract ore more easily. The dancers believed that given sufficient time, new flint, or ore, grew and matured into precious flint or metal, in the womb of the Earth Mother. Myths taught them this.

The second example is that of a *shaman*, or medicine man, who jumps over and around the sick person or animal he wants to cure by bringing the lost soul of the patient back to its body. But as he does not trust spirits to act of their own accord, he shows the lost soul, through sympathetic magic, what he wants it to do – which is to re-enter the body of the invalid, so that body and soul are reintegrated and can live to the full as before.

The third example is taken from the Siberian shamans who leap astonishingly high, even when wearing their heavy ritual costumes, often weighing up to thirty kilograms. These leaps into the air represent their *ascension to heaven*. These shamans also perform amazingly complicated steps in their ritual dances to induce *ecstacy*.

The final example is taken from classical antiquity. In the temples of Zeus Bromios (the Lord of the dark, rain-laden sky), a heavy fleece, cut into a pointed oval to represent the vagina of the Earth Mother, was brought out with singing and dancing in dry spells, so as to induce the god to mate with the Earth Mother and to fertilise her with the seed of his *rain*. A similar custom takes place in Arnhem Land in Australia, even now. In Australia, however, the Earth Mother is an ancestral figure.

I have used the word *ecstacy* in connection with shamans. It is hard to explain the word in modern terms. One has to use the terms of the psychology of magic. According to this doctrine, the shaman has to make a connection between the spirits on whose help he relies and his patient. This can only be done by emotion of high intensity, a kind of trance known as ecstasy, in which state the shaman can form the bridge between spirits and patient. Modern man also knows ecstasy, in religious fervour, or in love, or in aesthetic admiration, but the difference between a shaman and modern man lies in the fact that a shaman *directs* the mana which radiates from him in a state of ecstacy, whereas modern man 'drifts' on his emotional wave. Thus, the shaman consciously controls the whole process of emotion, ecstasy and mana and remains master of these psychic forces, whereas modern man is driven by them.

As Professor Eliade pointed out, shamanism is a technique of ecstasy, and this ecstasy has created many a dance figure and step.

How did myths originate?

They are the *theology* of early man, evolved from the experience of shamans in their ecstatic journeys to heaven and hell. During their ecstasies, the shamans described the spirits they saw and the landscapes they passed through on these journeys.

Where do legends stand?

Legends are a deterioration of myth and they could be called the *hagiology* of early man, attached to individual heroes, war heroes or culture heroes.

FIGURES FOUND IN FOLK DANCE

From the few examples we have just mentioned, we see that folk dance originated from the beliefs and faiths of primitive man. Folk dances were composed of steps and figures which had a practical intention. Early man made symbols for the most important things in his life. Symbols were understood by all, long before writing was ever devised. A symbol is much shorter than having to write out something. For example, everyone knows what a white flag means, or in Europe what thumbs up means, or a crown of laurels. The gods of early man were also believed to understand what was required of them, from the symbols shown by man.

Let us glance at some of these figures.

The circle represented either the moon disc (later the sun disc or the wheel) or the wheel of life and/or the unity of the community, and in some cases a protective circle used as a defence against evil spirits. The circle is a favourite in all countries. At times small circles are formed, at times very large ones, and in some cases, as in the *Sardanas* of Cataluña (eastern Spain), concentric circles are formed. However, they are all figures of the sun. In some dances of Mallorca, for example, each dancer draws a circle around himself or herself with the forefinger, while turning sunwise for luck. This is usually to protect oneself from evil influences, or from some disaster. Witches are reputed to do the same to this day.

The square is a symbol of the fact that man and woman are opposites yet complementary, and both are necessary for the continuance of the family. Son and daughter complete the square, ensuring the 'safety' or continuity of the family.

The diamond or *lozenge* is a symbol of '*regressus ad uterum*' and therefore of re-birth. This was extremely important to early man. It is a symbol of creation or of new life. It is a feminine emblem, similar to the ellipse, but in geometrical form (as the zig-zag is to the wavy line, the water symbol). When partners face each other, one moves forward a little, diagonally to his left, retreats, then moves forward diagonally to his right and retreats. Thus the ground pattern is that of a lozenge. This figure occurs in Andalucia in the *Seguidillas Sevillanas*, in some Aragonese *Jotas*, in Valencian and Murcian dances, and in some northern dances (though it is rarer there).

This lozenge is recognisable all over the world, in textiles, pottery, jewellery, sculpture and ironwork, even to this day. It is so common that we do not even notice it. Some textiles and carpets carry a dot, or circle, in the centre of the lozenge; this is the 'new life' which archaic man asked for.

The 'V' shape. Many dances in Spain contain floor patterns in the shape of a capital V, and it is widespread and frequent in European dance generally. This is a form of bull's horns. Partners both face the same way and advance diagonally to the left, then retrace their steps and repeat the figure to the right. This is found in *Fandangos*, in the *Jota Valencia*, in the *Seguidillas Murcianas,* in the *Panaderos* and many others.

The triangle. In his book *The Forge and the Crucible*, Mircea Eliade says that the triangle was a sacred symbol of the Earth Mother goddess. He quotes W.F. Jackson Knight (in *Cumaean Gates*) as saying that the most sacred sanctuary of Hellenism was Delphi ('delph' meant 'uterus' in Greek.) According to Eliade, Pausanias speaks of a place in Argos called Delta which was considered the sanctuary of Demeter, but it was interpreted later by Fick and Eisler as the triangle meaning 'vulva', the matrix of Mother Earth. For the Greeks, says Pythagoras, a triangle represented woman. Eliade says that a similar symbolism is to be found in India.

The triangle also represented the pine tree – the maritime pine that grows along the Mediterranean coast. It provides edible kernels. In fact, that tree was the emblem of the Earth Mother on the eastern Mediterranean coast, so the triangle was her symbol. The triangle also meant 'new life' – father, mother and child. There are only a few dances in Spain that still have this symbol as a figure during the dance.

The snake figure – another basic symbol very frequent in European dances – represents water and is therefore a fertility symbol, essential to pastoral and agricultural communities.

When people hold hands to form a single line, the leader can make a ground pattern like the curves of a snake, symbolising the ripples of water.

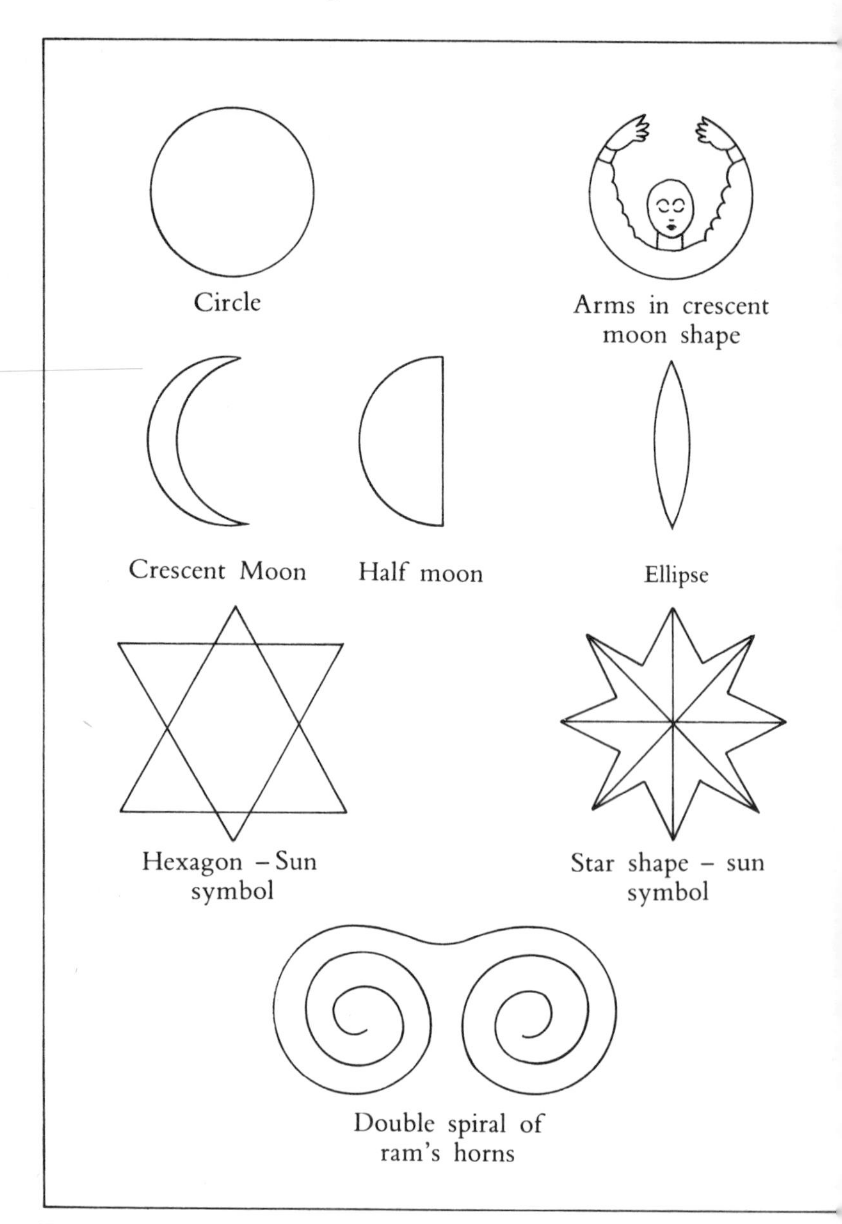

Figures
Their purpose is described in detail in the text; mostly, they are self-explanatory.

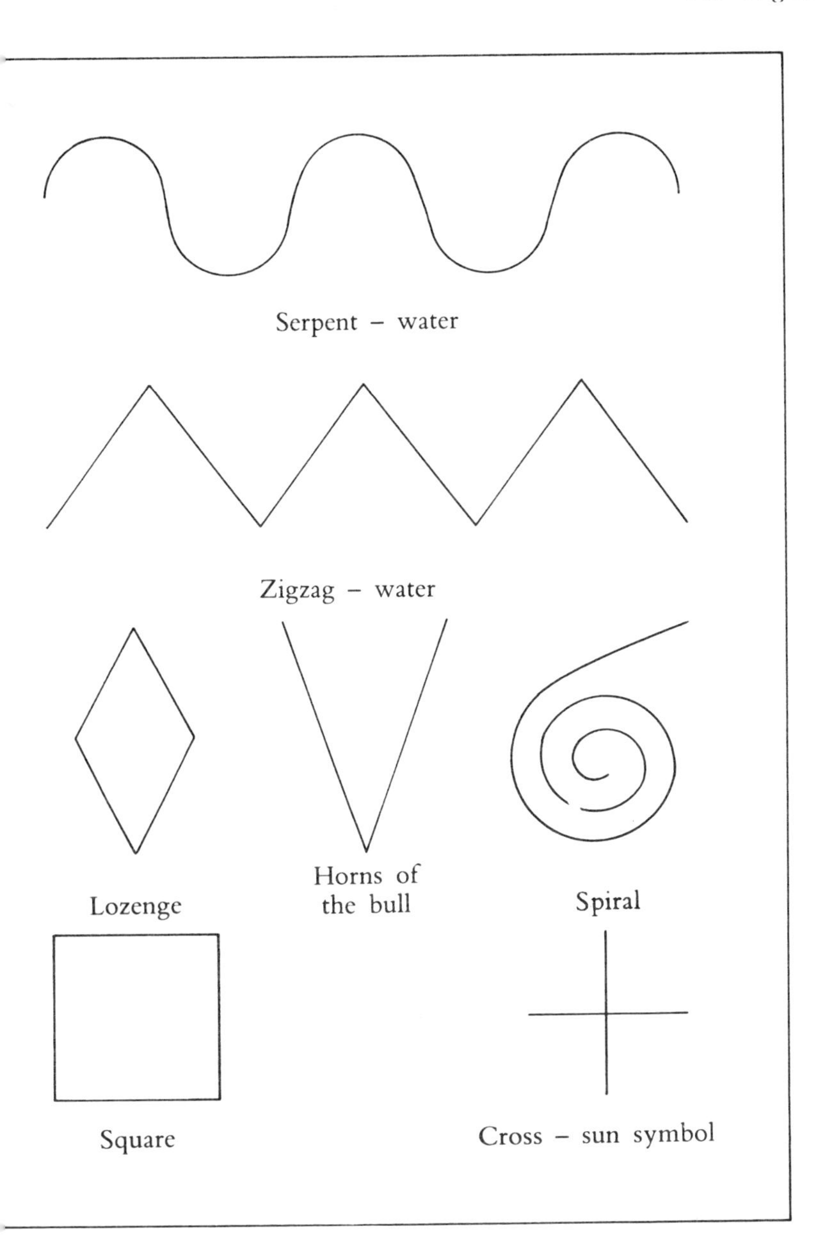
Serpent – water
Zigzag – water
Lozenge
Horns of
the bull
Spiral
Square
Cross – sun symbol

The figure of eight is another sacred symbol. It represents eternity, the renewal of life, completeness. Many loops may be involved. Such are the so-called 'Celtic' designs on monoliths, on jewellery and in Greek and Roman mural and floor patterns. Egyptian, classical and Near Eastern paintings and sculpture and mosaics contain this figure and it is to be seen in many Christian churches. The figure of eight originated from the sacred circle of the sun and that of life. The Euroboros snake with its tail in its mouth represented good luck, for it stood for the cycle of nature, the renewal of crops and pastures, so it was essential that once the circle came to an end it should automatically be renewed. To ensure good luck, therefore, the circle was doubled and the figure of eight was created: it meant 'eternity'. That is the reason why this figure occurs so frequently in Morris dances and many other ritual dances.

The zig-zag ground pattern can be performed in several ways. For example, by placing, say, the left foot to the side, the right foot across and in front of the left foot, stepping to the left again, placing the right foot behind the left foot, and so on, towards the left or towards the right, if one starts with the right foot to the right, etc. Another way which occurs in some Spanish dances is to step on left foot to the side (having started with both heels together), bring the right heel to the left, in front of the left foot, keeping the toe on the ground, then bring down the right heel, this being three beats of the music. Repeat the three movements according to the musical phrase. This can be done towards the right, by starting on right foot to the right side. In doing these steps man showed his deities what he required for his crops – the zig-zag and wavy line symbolise water. Another way of asking for rain which the Basques have kept up is leaping high into the air vertically and, while coming down, criss-cross the feet as many times as possible, thus representing lightning. (Lightning brings storms and storms bring rain.) King Louis XIV of France sent his dancing masters all over the countryside to collect steps and figures with which they could devise dances for social and theatrical purposes. This step was found and came to be called the 'entrechat'; it is still taught in ballet schools today, although few pupils know its significance.

The spiral is a symbol of creation. Man has eaten snails and shellfish for many thousands of years; many of them are now delicacies. The spiral of the snail's shell came to be a symbol of food or plenty. Many dances, both ritual and social, have kept this figure, in both European countries and parts of the East. In Provence and in Cataluña, at Christmas and on other feast days, lamps are made by putting a wick in a snail shell and filling the shell with oil. The shells are put in wet mud which is stuck in dabs on a ramp of steps, say, or along a path in a garden, or on a bannister or window sill, where they are left to burn themselves out. Snails represent plenty as well as creation. In Provence on 25th March (an ancient spring festival) the silk workers also light wicks in snail shells and place these on rafts, which are taken away by the current of a river.

The cross represents the sun as well as the circle and so is a sacred figure. Argentine peasants (the Pampas Indians) still decorate their pottery with a design showing the body of an ostrich with a cross within a circle. These Indians had noticed that before rain comes, ostriches spread out their wings and dance round, so they imagined that the ostriches brought rain; hence the designs of the cross and the circle (the sun) and an ostrich (rain bringer).

Early man had also seen that the sun rose in the east (land of birth), and set in the west (land of death); its zenith was in the south (land of fulness) and its opposite was in the north (absence of sun). The opposing poles were joined by a line, so the cross was created. The cross also represented the cosmos, because it covered the main directions of the compass. The four-pointed cross was one of the reasons why 'four' was a sacred number. Another reason was that four represented the father, the mother, the son and the daughter – emblems of the continuity of the family. To make sure of good luck, four was doubled, making eight. Four and eight are both numbers of the sun. Eight is a number popular among ritual dancers: six and eight men take part in what we call Morris dances (inherited from the early agriculturalists in Mesopotamia, 'the land between the two rivers', viz. the Tigris and the Euphrates, where crops were first grown, according to the authorities).

Now why six? Simply because early man noticed that to bring forth new life there would always be a father, a mother, and a child (new life), so three was a sacred number. In the ancient Near East, a triangle represented the Earth Mother. To make certain of good luck three was doubled to make six.

In dances, another way of making a cross figure is for four dancers to hold right hands in the centre of a square and dance sunwise (clockwise, since the hands of our clocks were made to imitate the direction of the course of the sun). If the dancers make a half-turn, hold left hands and move anti-clockwise it is a representation of the moon, the moon being the opposite of the sun and also the deity of the night.

A Far Eastern figure of the cross is what is called the *swastika* or hooked cross. If the extra strokes are on the right of the ends of the cross the figure revolves moonwise (anti-sunwise). I only know of one dance in which this swastika figure is preserved and that is in a Portuguese fishermen's dance called *A Tirana*. (The 'tyrant' presumably refers to the fisherman's sweetheart, who is always in the man's thoughts. She will not let him rest from thinking of her.)

Stars are also depicted in some folk dances, now incorporated into social dances.

The arches are hoops decorated with natural or paper flowers. Teams, usually of eight men, perform a dance like our Bacup Coconut Dancers. Provence, the Basque region, Italy and some northern Spanish villages have arches.

Usually the captain is raised on the arches at the end of the dance (except in Marseilles, where women dance it!) It seems that the raising of the captain always symbolised a human sacrifice, for many such dances end in the 'decapitation' or killing of the captain. Fenestrelle, Aubagne, Ibio and Marquina (northern Spain) have such dances. Dances without arches also have this killing of the captain, as in Britain.

The crescent moon is also an important figure in folk dance. It represents not only birth, but also the growing strength of the night deity, water (rain), and the horns of the sacred bull god. Many dances have retained this crescent-shaped figure. For example when partners face, then cross over to opposite sides/places, facing their partner all the time, this traces a half moon or a crescent as a ground pattern. In Spain it is still called the *media luna*, the half moon. The crescent is still a favourite figure in the Far East, in the Middle East, where it is a symbol of Islam (as testified by the Turkish flag), and in India. It is depicted on pottery and in jewellery, sculpture, textiles, embroidery, as well as in dance. Because the meaning of this figure is not generally known any longer, dancers tend to cross over in a straight line and even neglect to look at their partner as they cross!

In the whole of the Iberian Peninsula (except Cataluña on the eastern coast) the arms are held up above the head, curved, and a little forward to represent the crescent moon, and also the horns of the bull god (a very tiring position for the arms until one gets used to it!) The bull, as progenitor of the herd, was worshipped in Asia as well as in Europe. Even with the dawn of Christianity Mithraism thrived until the Roman Emperor Constantine was converted to Christianity, whereupon eventually Mithraism died out. (There is an ancient Mithraic temple in the City of London, built by the Romans.) So the arms in a crescent position also depict the horns of the sacred bull. It was surprising to me at first, when I saw so many Virgin Mary statues with a crescent moon at the foot and in some cases the horns of a bull, such as in Santo

Domingo de Silos (south of Burgos in Spain) and in a small church in Paris, including the Patroness of the Spanish Basques, also Our Lady of Aranzazu, who is at the same time a tree goddess, for she stands in a tree.

The ellipse is a figure to promote creation or new life. It is not as frequent as the half moon, but it still exists in dances. Partners will cross over to opposite places and go back to their own place, but facing each other all the time and in a much straighter line than for the half moon, which must of course be semi-circular. The ellipse is a feminine symbol and during the thirteenth and fourteenth centuries AD was used to frame Christos Pantokrator – as seen in the smaller towns in parts of France. It means birth or re-birth.

CHAPTER TWO

Various kinds of dance and their aims

IT IS NOT YET REALISED by the majority of people that modern ballet can be created by one brain, but it has taken many generations of brains to create one folk dance. This is brought home to you forcefully while you watch Spanish and Portuguese folk dances. Not all of them, of course, because some are comparatively recent or else modernised, but most of them make you gasp and wonder whoever invented such an intricate rhythm or such unusual complicated figures. Yes, who? Ballet choreographers and musicians constantly refer to folk music or folk dance for inspiration for steps, themes and figures. Well they may! Folk dance and music are an inexhaustible wealth of artistic treasures. Many have drunk deep at the never-failing fountains of traditional music and dance.

The Iberian Peninsula is rich in traditions and a splendid place for inspiration. Each province has its own characteristics, its own style of performance, rhythms and music. The music, of course, is greatly influenced by ethnic invasions as well as from the material available in the environment. The dances are evolved from the ethnic background – of the invaders as well as the people already in the region. Whenever a particular tribe settled in a district, its own traditions were amalgamated with those of the existing inhabitants. The climate and topography also play an important role in style and the choice of figures for, of course, costume is adapted to the climate and that influences the style of dance and movements, too.

AIMS OF FOLK DANCE

What prompted the dances to be created? There are several aims. Early man knew that dance brought euphoria to those taking part, just as birds, insects, elephants, snakes, monkeys and apes do. Many animals dance for joy – dolphins are a prime example. There is often a purpose too: mostly for mating, but also (as in the case of bees) to indicate where food lies. A baby who cannot yet walk will respond to the rhythm of song or any music by bobbing up and down in joy.

So, to bring the community together man created *community dances* in which all joined in. All felt happy, all were equal who took part. These community dances are mainly circular or in a wavy line formation where all join hands, or else they stand in two rows facing partners. Often these are progressive dances; that is, couples will change places by one partner moving in a sideways direction to face a new partner then moving back to face the original partner. This changing of partner for very short periods appears to be so as to enable young people to meet others in the dance, and thus remove some of the shyness that prevents young people from easily mixing with others on an equal footing. It also gives people the opportunity of meeting other people beside their own partner.

Courting dances are specifically for enabling young people to keep their partner for the duration of the dance. This type is important in a community where the sexes are separated by their daily work, and so have little opportunity to meet. In the north of the Peninsula the young men have to show off their agility and resistance in the dances, to show that they would make a good husbandman, for in the north matriarchy lasted for thousands of years longer than in the south, where it is the woman who has to show off her dexterity and charm to woo the man, who is the ruler, the chief, and where patriarchy is the norm. There are all manner of dances and customs linked to marriage. A modified form of ceremonial intercourse was practised in ancient Egypt by the Pharaoh and his queen, and until recently in the furrows in some villages of Cataluña, eastern Spain, where a bride and groom with their attendant dancers were the protagonists in special sowing rites. These included a meal, spinning round like tops, the feet touching partner's feet, ritual dances, and ploughing and sowing ceremonies (according to Aurelio Capmany Farrés).

On the Mediterranean coast, the *orange* is the sun emblem as well as the symbol of marriage. It is used in festivals of spring and regeneration of the year, and in some parts of the Southern Balkans young men bring an orange to their partner as an invitation. The custom of orange blossom for a bride's head-dress, or her bouquet, comes from this belief. When Charles V of Spain conquered the Netherlands, many southern customs were brought north, including the custom in Binche, Belgium, of throwing oranges to the crowd during their spring festivals, which are extremely impressive. The dancers have to jump for hours on end during the procession, to entice crops to grow tall. They also throw oranges at the crowd 'for luck'.

Therapeutic dances are another type, performed only by the medicine men or leaders of the tribe – the initiated ones. This type is still practised in the Balkans, in parts of Africa and Australia, in America and parts of the world where sophisticated western methods of medicine are not used. The medicine man leaps over the sick – be he animal or human – from side to side, chanting and calling on the spirit of the sick to come back and cure its owner. In Italy, the *Tarantella* is said originally to have been one of those dances. Certainly it is a fact that lively music or movement can help a sick person to feel better. Hospitals encourage dance groups to come and perform in the wards, for patients respond to dance and music. Several people have told me that they feel much better when groups come and perform dances or jolly music. They feel elated and forget their troubles. Early man knew that.

We still have in Europe some *teaching dances* for young children; for example, 'This is the way we wash our hands', etc. All European countries had, or still do have, this sort of dance, for children to learn through mime, music and rhyme.

Men's dances. The young men of the tribe who hunted, or fished, had to learn agility, resistance to fatigue and discipline, not only to procure food, but also to defend the tribe. Unity of purpose and obedience were essential. This type of dance still exists in many parts of the world, such as the Balkans, Greece, Turkey, Africa – to my certain knowledge, for I have seen them – but also probably in other parts of the world too. The modern tendency of mixing men and women in all the dances, regardless of their original intent, only goes to show the ignorance that prevails, for women have no part in this type of dance, any more than men have a part in girls' dances round a well-head to ask for a husband. Turkey, for example, has some stalking dances for hunters and some partridge-mating dances which only men should dance because of their ritual content, but girls join in nowadays, just as some Morris sides in our country admit women, although these ritual dances were originally strictly only for men.

Ritual dances are a vast subject. Religious or ritual dances were evolved by archaic man to ensure enough food for the family or community. Without sufficient food they would all perish. As a hunter-gatherer, man required animals to feed on, or fruit, or nuts in plenty to tide over till the following year. He evolved ways of attaining his aim through sympathetic magic, or by miming his wishes to show his deities what was required of them. These ritual dances had to be performed in a quiet place. Hence he sought caves, or high mountain tops. In the caves we can still see paintings of the animals he wished to hunt for food, for example in Altamira in Spain, in Lascaux, France, in Northern Italy, Scandinavia and other places, where he danced and chanted in seclusion, to ensure good hunting and gathering. Fishermen also dance, simulating fish caught in a net and struggling to escape. This occurs on the Black Sea coast, in north-east Greece and Malaya. It shows the fish that they must allow themselves to be caught in the nets. Fishermen often do this on the decks of their fishing smacks – and with conviction too! It must have been the initiated or medicine men who taught and performed these dances originally, for these rites were too sacred to be performed by everyone; a priesthood was evolved and these men had to undergo special training, as they still do today.

It is revealing to watch ritual dances from Europe, from the Far East and from the islands near India and to see that most of these dances have similar figures. The steps may be different, the music and costumes, even the instruments may differ, but the figures are similar and in many cases exactly the same as those of our Morris Men. How did this come about?

As the Neolithic peoples evolved the cultivation of grain, so did they create dances to ensure good crops. Rain and sun were necessary. As the Neolithic people moved westward and eastward in search of more land to cultivate, they took their customs and knowledge with them. So it is reasonable to suppose that they must have had a common origin, which must have been centred between the rivers Tigris and Euphrates, since this is where the cultivation of cereals is reputed to have started. Priests danced sacred dances to promote the crops. These were called the Korybantes in the Near East, and the Kouretes in Crete. Later the Salii (priests of Rome) also danced 'for full jars' as they said. All food was stored in enormous earthenware jars in those days, to protect them from rats, mice and the elements. (An American scientist has discovered 'primitive' wheat – emmer

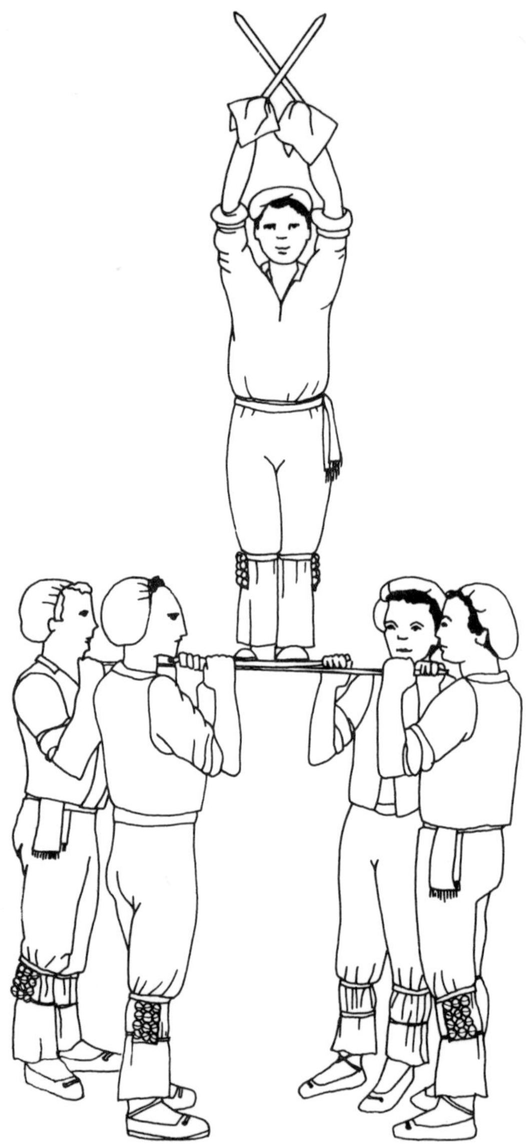

Basque Sword Dance
The surrogate captain is hoisted on cross swords, in a similar fashion to the English sword dancers. This kind of performance is found in various parts of Spain, not only among the Basques.

and einkorn—growing wild in central Anatolia. Some authorities also believe that wild wheat grew in parts of Egypt.) Another remarkable fact is that the number of dancers were eight, six or five, which corresponds to the numbers usual in Europe for ritual dances today. There is an exception, and that is when twelve men dance a ritual dance such as is performed in Ibio, in northern Spain. Each dancer holds a wooden spear and at the end of the dance they form a lock or platform on which the surrogate king mounts, is raised to shoulder level, and is then pierced by the sword of the real captain, as he falls to the ground. The act of piercing is, of course, mimicked nowadays. A marine conch and drum provide the accompaniment. Most eerie. The twelve dancers here represent the thirteen lunations of the solar year; the surrogate is the thirteenth, who has to die for the good of the community. Sacrificial dances of this type are also found among our own Morris dances, and on the island of Korçula in the Adriatic, but of course in a modified form. Death and resurrection dances are frequent in Europe. The Basques are excellent exponents of this type of dance. Naturally, these dances represent the renewal of vegetation and of nature in spring after the winter sleep; this occurs also in other countries in the mummers' plays.

There are many places in Spain where men perform ritual dances in churches, one specific case being in Seville Cathedral. For some reason this is quoted frequently, whereas many other places where dances take place in churches are not mentioned, with very rare exceptions and these by folklorists only. In 586 AD, in the celebrated Third Council of Toledo, dancing in churches was prohibited as 'pagan' and in 1777 Charles III of Spain ordered that dancing and singing of pagan origin be prohibited in churches and cathedrals. But the custom was so firmly established that they never stopped dancing and singing in many churches. (This is fortunate for us.) In Santiago de Compostela, 'Giants' dance; in Santo Domingo de Silos the

Morris Men dance before the Virgin Mary in the church; and in Cantabria, the Picayos (ritual dancers) perform in churches, in front of them and at country sanctuaries, as in many other towns and villages. In Santo Domingo de Silos, the statue of Our Lady is carried to the square where several dances are performed before her, including a maypole dance, the ribbons being plaited by the ritual dancers.

Dance was also a means of expressing sentiments such as supplication for success in an enterprise, joy, thanksgiving for favours received – either from man or from nature – and requests for favours, such as good crops and plenty of food. Through ritual dances man worked his 'magic', and thus assured himself of success.

ANIMALS LINKED TO RITUAL AND DANCE

Animals, particularly domesticated animals like goats, sheep, cattle and horses, often become almost a deity and have at times been linked with ritual dances.

The *goat god Pan* gradually travelled north, with his pan pipes, to call spring and the return of nature's growth after a winter's sleep. The satyrs of ancient Greece are examples of this deity. In England he is known as the Green Man.

In Staffordshire we have the yearly September *deer dance* at Abbot's Bromley, where six men, carrying reindeer skulls complete with antlers, dance in front of farmsteads and in the village. They bring good luck and plenty to men and animals and ensure good crops for the coming year. They are accompanied by the Man-Woman, a Boy with 'lazy-tongs' (representing lightning which brings rain), a cross-bowman and a Fool.

Bulls. It is small wonder that the bull was deified, because man depended on his herds before and even during the agricultural era, for his food. The ancient Minoans in Crete evolved bull worship and the sacrifice of the deity in their own special way. Acrobats 'played' the bull and jumped over and on to it, before the killing took place. Traces of this 'play' can still be discerned in the bullfighting of Spain, Portugal and southern France. Although the Romans brought Mithraism to those parts of Europe which they ruled, very little trace of bull worship is to be found, except in Ireland, where Celtic priests drank its blood (like the Egyptians) to forecast oracles. We also have innumerable public houses called 'The Bull', 'The Bull and Bush' or 'The Black Bull' to remind us of the importance of this animal.

According to the records of the Presbytery of Dingwall, bulls were sacrificed in the parish of Gairlech in Ross-shire and oblations of milk poured on the hills as late as 1640 (Spence, *The Mysteries of Britain*).

Spence also quotes from the *Chronicle of Lanercost* Book II, viii: that pagan rites in Scotland were regarded as 'common usage' is rendered clear enough in a passage from which it appears that John, the parish priest of Inverkeithing, Fife, was cited before his bishop in 1262 for having celebrated Easter Week 'according to the rites of Priapus' by collecting the maidens of the town and making them dance around the figure of the phallic deity, singing the while. He pleaded the 'common usage' of the country, and was allowed to retain his benefice. On page 165 one reads . . . 'It (the mistletoe) was culled on the sixth day of the moon. Extraordinary preparations for feast and sacrifice were made beneath the tree which bore it, says Pliny, and two white bulls whose horns had never been bound were conveyed thither . . . A white-clad Druid climbed the tree and cut the mistletoe with a golden sickle. As it fell it was caught in a white cloth. The bulls were then sacrificed and prayers offered up to the god.'

Bull cults were well established in Ireland and Scotland by the first century AD. The traditional Ulster hero Cuchulain was associated with the Brown Bull. In this strange saga the central episode is the 'War of the Bulls'. They fought between the armies of Queen Maeve and her husband King Ailell.

Today in Spain during the summer when the bulls fight best, numerous bullfights are organised and the atmosphere is electric. If a village is too poor to buy bulls for killing, then tamer, older bulls are brought into the plaza and 'played' by the young bloods of the village. These are then driven off to another village, where the same thing happens again. These bulls are called *vaquillas* (heifers), but of course they are not! In some villages hobby-bulls are paraded around the village. In some places where real bullfights take place, rockets or fireworks are fixed to the horns of the animals, to make them fierce, they say. They certainly are infuriated . . . if not terrified.

In India *the sacred cow* is still worshipped in several ways. The ancient Egyptians believed that the sacred cow had given birth to all their gods. As time evolved their beliefs, the sacred cow became anthropomorphic and the cow goddess was called Hathor, yet she retained her cow's head and curved horns in some cases. A few statuettes represent her with a cow's body at the back and woman's form in front, still carrying the curved horns of the sacred cow. Hathor also represents the moon goddess and her curved horns are the crescent moon. In Portugal, near the western coast, in Cascais, once a year a bull is drugged and paraded through the streets with flowered garlands round its neck. Women and girls come and touch him, rubbing themselves against his sides and calling him 'Little Mark', thus hoping for good luck in the guise of a husband or of children. The emblem of St Mark is a bull.

In the province of Guadalajara (León) a man dresses up as a hobby cow with a bull's mask and has a following of youths in sheepskins carrying large bells round their waists. These followers pretend to kill the vaquilla (hobby cow) and drink 'its blood' in the guise of wine. This custom of parading the streets in a group in animal disguises appears to have existed among the Persians of old, too.

The horse is another sacred animal. It was man's first means

Hobby Horse

This type of hobby horse is autochthonous in Valcarlos, Navarre. In the Soule Valley, France, in Tardeta and neighbourhood, the horse is the same as this one, and is glorious! He wears a red bodice and a white lace skirt, with gold embroideries. He is a man-woman. The artificial flowers covering his hat represent spring. The skirt is lace.

of locomotion, apart from his own two legs. Anyone who had a tame horse had plenty. It is still considered a sacred symbol. Hobby-horses are used in British Morris dances, in the Basque country, in Provence, as well as in the Iberian Peninsula. The horseshoe is still an emblem of luck in many parts of Europe and people nail one on, or near, their front door, points upward, to 'keep the luck'. (This horseshoe is connected with the crescent moon, another emblem of luck.)

In Central America, Mexico, in places like La Quebrada de Humahuaca, in Puna Jujena Abrapampa, Casabindo, Ronconada and Santa Catalina, hobby-bulls and hobby-horses take part in official festivals. For San Juan (mid-summer), *Los Plumados* (the Feathered Ones) are Indians, who have sworn to dance for favours such as the recovery of lost animals and the curing of diseases. These *Plumados* wear ostrich feather head-dresses and dance very slowly. They wear masks and dance day and night. Feathers are woven into the borders of their clothes – the head-dress being secured to the hat. They carry a bull's head and a horse's head, both being very important features for fertility of the fields. They are called *torito* and *caballito* respectively ('little bull' and 'little horse'). The masks are fixed to the breasts of the wearers. Now, since the horse is said not to have been known there before the Spaniards came to America, and both these fertility rites are well known in Europe, it is possible that these customs were brought over to America from Europe.

The eagle. Early man noticed that of all the birds that flew in the sky, the eagle flew highest, therefore this bird became the sun-bird, the highest, the most powerful. There are ritual eagle dances in Spain that are performed only at special celebrations, such as midsummer festivals. Berga, north of Barcelona, is famous for its wonderful festivals that contain numerous symbolic dances and rituals. The 'Eagle' there wears Elizabethan costume, a hobby-eagle body and head. He scratches the ground ritually, then turns round and round sunwise. His assistant, dressed like him but without the

EAGLE
In the midsummer festival of Berga the eagle is the bird of the sun. He turns round and round to show the sun what it must do.

eagle's body, sees that he does not tumble. Young boys crowd round the eagle as it turns, then they try to avoid being touched by the bird (although if it touches them it brings good luck!) Mallorca also has its own eagles, so does Cataluña, but the dances there are quite different from those of Berga.

The Romans (and even earlier the Assyrians) considered the eagle as an emblem of supreme power, for their emperors had double-headed eagles on their person, on their ensigns, and on their coins. Even in recent times emperors took double-headed eagles as their emblems.

Other animals could bring good luck, such as the *cock*, symbol of virility, the *pig* (for many millenia, in the vast forests of Europe, man depended on pigs for food, and the swineherd was the wise man of the tribe), the *bear* (at the approach of spring the bear comes out of hibernation; today men still believe the bear brings spring). In many mountainous regions men dance in the street dressed as a bear to help the coming of spring. The *snake* is a fertility symbol, as is the horn; for the bull's horn meant fertility and still symbolises good luck.

HORNS AND HEAD-DRESSES

Horned animals played an important part in the life of hunters among archaic peoples. Man made tools, toggles and ornaments in horn and bone for thousands of years. Reindeer and wild (later domesticated) cattle, as well as sheep and goats, provided man with valuable food, so these animals became sacred. Symbols of horns, meaning plenty (hence 'cornucopia'), were devised in most parts of the world. Christian bishops wear mitres which may have originated from the fish head-dresses of the Sumerian priesthood (meaning power and plenty, for fish have innumerable eggs, so fish meant plenty). They may also have symbolised two horns in a stylised form. Both these interpretations mean fertility and regeneration. We have reliefs from Sumeria depicting priests wearing the fish body down their back, the head being worn as a crown. Some mummers and ritual dancers today still wear a mitre-style head-dress, such as the mummers of Dungeer, in Kinross in Ireland.

Ram's horns. When sheep were first domesticated, it must have taken a long time for man to come to a full understanding of animal husbandry, but he early realised the importance of the ram for the increase of the flock, so the ram was deified. The Egyptians also deified the ram, and exquisite stone rams are to be seen in the British Museum, carved by early Egyptian artists. These statues are perfect in every detail. The ram's horns have come down to us in sculpture, as the horns of the 'Green Man', whose effigies can be admired also in ceramics. In folk dances it is preserved as a 'cast off ' figure. Ram's horns were symbolic because they also represented the spiral, so these symbols merged in the progress of time.

Flocks of goats were also domesticated by man, but the billy-goat became associated with the flute or pipe and therefore with music and not with dance. The great god Pan was renowned for his pan-pipes, which are still played in north-western Spain, Portugal, the mountainous parts of Cataluña and parts of the Balkans, as well as in northern South America.

Head-dress ritual. According to the famous anthropologist Professor Edmund Leach of Cambridge University, the wearing of tall pointed hats among ritual dancers is an effort to remind the Earth Mother to 'get busy' and 'do her duty' to get plants and seeds to grow. The tall pointed hat represented the phallus and helped Mother Earth to bring forth new life. This is, of course, an ancient belief, but the custom of wearing tall pointed hats by ritual dancers has lasted to our day. Examples are the Mevlevi or turning dervishes of Turkey, who wear tall pointed hats with round tops, called by the same name as a phallus. Numerous chiefs as well as dancers in many countries wear a tall hat or extravagant head-dress to denote power and in some cases to show that the wearer possesses exceptional force and/or wisdom; this wisdom must be stored in an extra space, like Buddha, whose images make him wear an extra boss on top of his head to show he has more wisdom than other people.

In his article in the *Revista de Dialectologia y Tradiciones Populares* Chapters 1–2, Julio Caro Baroja describes how in

Almonacid del Marquesando, in the province of Cuenca, Spain, on 2nd and 3rd February (San Blas), ritual dancers come out dressed as devils, and parade through the town ringing huge cowbells – up to half a yard long – attached to their waist. The bells are fixed to a harness worn over a pierrot-like flowered costume. The devils drive out 'evil spirits' from the town during the morning, when they wear the 'gorra de la Virgen' (the Virgin's cap) and in the afternoon they change and wear the 'gorra de San Blas'. The morning headgear looks just like an extremely tall bowler hat made up of paper flowers attached to a wire frame. This frame is shaped like a phallus. The San Blas hat is a very tall red mitre made of cardboard edged with tinsel, and sometimes a gold cross is fixed on the front. The colour red signifies the colour of life, and the mitres appear to have attached to themselves a similar meaning to the morning caps (fertility). Each 'devil' holds a staff to help him walk and sway his body back and forth, in order to cause the bells on his back to clang. The purpose is common all over Europe: noise drives away evil influences and the 'whifflers' try to purify the neighbourhood before the coming of the new year and new growth. The devils of Almonacid also carry sceptres with the mask of a devil's face and the face of San Blas on the back of the head. These 'devils' take part in religious processions, along with a second group of dancers called the 'endiablados' (bedevilled ones) who are really Morris dancers as we know them in England. This team of dancers also have a maypole dance with the weaving of coloured ribbons round the pole (the world tree) and a stick dance followed by a plough dance, during the course of which a plough is assembled from several parts brought on by the dancers. Their last dance is a sword dance.

Stick and sword dances are widely performed in Spain and nowadays are connected with religious festivals. Since the Christian church could not eradicate these powerful traditions, the dances were incorporated into church festivals and performed in the traditional manner so long as a Christian saint was adopted as patron of the day and church attendance kept up.

The question arises, why do the Almonacid ritual dancers wear two kinds of headgear? If we follow Professor Edmund Leach's reasoning, we may interpret the two kinds of head-dress in the following way: the tall rounded (morning) hat is a phallic symbol which, associated with the Earth Mother (nowadays the Virgin Mary) will bring good crops in the coming year. The mitre or fishhead, the tall split hat, denotes the power of the fish to create many new offspring. The pope wears a triple-tiara crown (also a phallic symbol) meaning that the wearer is omnipotent. Cardinals do not wear tall hats, for they carry out orders. So one could say that there had to be the duality (male-female) potency on Candlemas Day, representing what was required, i.e. new life: the devils to drive away evil; the sword dance, with its sun-symbol figures, asking the orb to ripen crops; the maypole dance with its tree of life emblem, carrying the colours of all three realms (heaven, earth and the under-world), thus uniting the whole universe.

In Guipuzcoa, the Basque country, some February ritual dancers also wear tall pointed hats decorated with paper flowers. They carry an apple in each hand and dance a stick dance in many parts of the town, also to ensure fertility of crops. Their *sagar dantza* (apple dance) is performed from early morning on, even if the inhabitants are still in bed and there is no one to see them.

Other parts of Spain also have these festivals, as in Aragón and at Verin, Galicia, where fishhead or mitre headgear is also worn.

A full account of the significance of the horn is given in Elworthy, pages 73–74 (see Bibliography). He quotes many instances of the use of horns in Italy today, and belief in their potency against evil and other calamities. For example, in Naples Museum there is an Assyrian relief of a priest wearing

Sagar Dantza (Apple Dance)
The apple dancer and his three companions carry an apple, which brings good luck, in each hand. It is the fruit of the North, of matriarchy and of the moon. His headdress represents spring because of the multi-coloured artificial flowers.

a mitre shaped like a pair of horns. In the same city most butchers' shops have a pair of bullock's or ram's horns over the doorway for luck. They are usually painted red and white. Fruiterers and grocers also have a pair, somewhere in public view, or even a single bull horn on the wall. Hotels and other public buildings keep a single polished horn mounted on a stand, as a common ornament. In Zurich, a pair of stone horns, set up in a crescent shape, is exhibited: they are supposed to have been made for the same purpose. At Taranta, Italy, an ancient Greek cow's horn, also of stone, can be seen. In many countries horn is used for amulets, for good luck. 'Corno', in Italian argot, means phallus as well as horn, and is the most powerful prophylactic, especially the 'corne torse': all charms are called 'corno'. Elworthy shows illustrations of Greek and Roman tombs of ancient times protected by a pair of horns.

The African continent also holds similar beliefs. Gods and chiefs wear horned or tall head-dresses, either in metal, wood, or feathers. The Yorubas wear these head-dresses to denote generative power. Their god Elcgby wears a calabash in the form of a phallus on his head, for he brings fertility. His sceptre, or club, is similarly shaped. He represents the worship of the Earth Mother – she is called Ea. Twins are worshipped as the duality of life – opposites making a whole. A phallus among them is called an 'ogo'; the same word is used for 'power' and 'penis'.

Some Celtic tribes also wore two horns on their helmets to show prowess.

The ancient Americans also wore tall head-dresses to denote power, chieftaincy and vision, as the Aztec paintings show us. In Europe in the Middle Ages, knights wore bunches of ostrich feathers on their helmets to show superior rank.

SYMBOLS USED IN RITUAL DANCES

Not only in the animal kingdom but also the plant kingdom adds enrichment to the rituals, customs and dances in various ways.

Trees have always been venerated by early man. They were his first shelter, and in his gratitude he endowed them with souls; indeed, to him every tree, plant, stone, animal, bird or reptile had a soul – a spirit. As we have seen, before killing an animal or cutting down a tree, ritual chants and dances were performed to explain to the spirit of the proposed victim why the deed had to be done. After the act more ritual chants and dances were performed to appease the spirit of the victim and ask it not to take vengeance against the perpetrators of the act.

Some trees, like the willow, were considered as promoting fertility, so women who wanted babies would embrace the trunk of the tree and ask for children. In France, up to the last century, this ritual was still carried out in some provinces. (See Frazer's *Golden Bough.)*

In some parts of Europe, including Britain, when a child is born, a tree is planted. It used to be believed that the child's life was connected with that of the tree, and so injury inflicted on the one would naturally react on the other.

Some trees were considered to have curative powers, so if a child had rickets it was passed through a hole made in the trunk of a sacred tree, like a beech, oak or willow. This custom was carried out in various parts of Europe and in Britain.

The custom of dancing round may trees stems from similar beliefs, for a tree meant regeneration of nature; those trees which bore edible fruit like the pear tree (a feminine tree) were especially venerated. The maypole is another form of the tree of spring, of life; the embodiment of the renewal or regeneration of nature. Some maypoles are crowned with flowers or shrubbery and carry items of food which are given as prizes in special competitions. Other maypoles have 8 to 16 ribbons of different colours attached to the top, the loose ends of the ribbons being held by dancers who dance round the tree or pole, intertwining the ribbons as they go. Then they go round in the opposite direction and untwine the

TREES *have been sacred emblems of life since prehistoric times. The pine is particularly common in the Near East and represents the Earth Mother goddess, and therefore fertility. The triangle is the stylised pine, representing the Earth Mother goddess as well.*

ribbons. The colour of each ribbon symbolically connects the dancer with a particular aspect of life. For example, red is for life and love; blue for purity and the heavens, green for the regeneration of nature, white is for purity and innocence, yellow and orange for the sun and for wisdom.

In some ritual performances such as the fire-walking ceremony at San Pedro Manrique, in Castile, the three 'Móndidas' (priestesses) have a tree planted in front of their house and decorated with natural and artificial flowers and streamers – as is described in a later chapter.

The early Greeks worshipped the god Priapus, whose emblem was a fig, but whose origin is lost in the mists of time. It was not an accident that Adam and Eve wore fig leaves in the Bible story. They were said to have worn the leaves out of modesty. It is much more likely that they wore them as emblems of future fructification. Figs are symbols of fertility in Cataluña still. In some festivals people call 'figa, figa' and throw figs or an imitation fig into the air – presumably to attract fertility in nature.

AGRICULTURAL RITUALS

The early cereal planters in Sumeria devised rituals to promote the growth of crops. They used *planting sticks* to strike a hole in Mother Earth, in order to drop some seeds into her, just as some South American Indians still do for their maize crops. The sticks became sacred and were phallic symbols. If struck together the sound would attract the attention of the spirits. These dances were performed by the wise men or medicine men of the tribe. When Neolithic man advanced westwards he brought the knowledge of cereal-growing with him, together with the appropriate rituals. Our Morris dancers are part of the heritage from those times. In Europe (apart from Scandinavia) and the Near, Middle and Far East similar dances are still performed, with practically the same figures, although the costumes, music and instruments are different according to the region. But it is astonishing to see such similarity in the dances. *Circles, the figure of eight, the cross over, diagonal patterns, casting off, spirals,* all come into the dances. Even the pads of bells worn on the legs to help waken the spirits, the sticks and swords, and in some cases the costume, are practically the same as for Morris dances. White denotes spirits. Blackened faces are used as a kind of mask, so as not to be recognised as one of the community, but as a spirit. In the Meseta of Spain (the central plateau), which is almost entirely devoted to agriculture, the ritual dancers all wear white, and many have frilly petticoats and skirts, to show they are the Androgyne (male/female beings; 'complete', since they have the propensities of both). Some ritual dances contain the figure of hitting the soil during the dance, to contact the earth – as in our Morris dance 'bean setting' and in some Basque dances with sticks – thus keeping contact with the earth spirits. There are other ways of keeping contact; in some dances of Spain and Portugal, dancers go down on one knee while bringing an arm round in a circular motion, the forefinger touching the ground as the arm goes round, then bringing both arms up above the head while rising from the kneeling position. Another way in the Basque country is called 'the drunkard'; in two facing rows, the dancers strike a wineskin brought by a ninth dancer who gallops from one end of the rows to the other, then falls to the ground. (This last movement is out of context; in reality the pigskin only replaces a goatskin, and what the dancers were doing in olden times was to force the evils of the past year into the animal skin so that the world should be purified before the new year came in. But the original meaning of the dance has been forgotten.)

Another problem that puzzles some people is why are six or eight men dancers associated with ritual dances (those we call Morris dances)? Other dances must be performed by five men only. Six and eight are numbers of the sun, while five is the number of the moon.

Ancient man was anxious to ensure the continuation of his family. He noticed that a father, a mother and a child made three. Hence three became an important number. A triangle became the symbol of three, but to make doubly sure of good luck he turned three into six – two triangles and the six-pointed star. Thousands of years ago the triangle was an emblem of the Earth Mother in the Near East. Six was then a sacred number.

On the other hand a complete family consisted of father, mother, son and daughter. Four became a sacred number as mentioned earlier: the square, or the cross. The cross has another meaning – that of the 'four directions' as some South American Indians call it. Since the sun rises in the east – land of birth – that is the first direction. It sets in the west – land of death – second direction. Its zenith is in the south, and opposite is the north – the four directions, so the cross, which meant the sun and the cosmos, was devised. The cross has been drawn in many countries since prehistoric times. But, to go back to number four, to ensure good luck for the family, four was doubled to make eight (a double sun number). Hence six and eight are numbers chosen for ritual dances for bringers of spring, for ritual dances that ensure good crops – whether they use sticks or swords.

Five is the number of the moon (the moon's fruit is an apple because when cut into two halves across, there are five divisions). Mining dances mainly have five performers, for mines are mostly dark, sunless places and therefore under the protection of the moon. Dances with five performers are always sword dances, whether in the Basque country or in our northern counties where rapper dances – using metal swords with a wooden handle at each end – are performed. Some of the rapper dances have arches, and both here and in Spain the dancers are obliged to dance very close together while they twist and untwist their swords or rappers. Since mines bring forth metal, it is logical that metal swords should be used, not sticks. Nevertheless, sword dances performed by men in a ritual manner for a ritual purpose are *agricultural* dances to promote good crops, not war dances. War dances are performed by *all* the young men of a community, not by six or eight people only; and they are designed to defend the tribe, therefore particular stress is put on attacking the foe and escaping thrusts from an enemy weapon, *not* in performing special figures to bring rain, sun, and a good height for the crops, as our Morris dances require.

While mentioning the triangle and number three as sacred, it has always been a wonder to me how the statues of the Virgin Mary in Spain mostly wear garments that are tight round the neck and become ever wider and more voluminous towards the hem, so she looks like a cone or triangle. No other country that I have visited has such costumes for the Virgin Mary. Is there an ancient Near Eastern influence here?

Particular movements are to be found the world over in ritual dances of all kinds. A leap or caper is a case in point.

Berriz Death and Resurrection Dancers
These ritual dancers in the Basque country enact the death and resurrection theme in several places. The captain in this case represents the death of winter and the two dancers kick high to show the crops how tall they must grow. After a short time the captain comes to life again. Different countries have, of course, several different ways of representing the death of nature and rejuvenation in spring – as in Britain.

These feature in our *Morris dances* and all sorts of ritual agricultural dances. It is very often used as a symbol of the height the crops need to grow to. The Basques kick very high, above the head even, in their ritual dances. The ritual dances are usually performed by groups of eight or six, the numbers of the sun. In some districts the number is doubled for good luck, so there are sixteen or twelve dancers.

We must not forget, however, that the leap or caper was also practised by the ancient priests of the Near East, the Korybantes, and those of Crete, the Kouretes, as well as the Roman priests called the Salii who 'leapt for full jars!' These earthenware jars were enormous containers in which grain, wine, and all sorts of foodstuffs were kept to protect them from mice and insects.

SWORD DANCES

As we have seen, an important agricultural ritual was the stick dance to promote fertility in the soil. These dances must, therefore, date back to the time when man first began to till the soil – about 5000 BC. When metal was discovered it was found that swords made a louder (and therefore more powerful) noise when clashed together than sticks did, so in areas where metal was available sword dances superseded stick dances.

Near and around mining districts people would be able to obtain swords much more easily than those who lived far away from mining sites. It seems clear then that metal swords could and would be used, near and around mining sites, and not so much far from these sites. This does not mean that swords came first, then sticks were substituted; on the contrary. Sticks were used for planting and were superseded by metal swords later.

In her book *Sword Dance and Drama* Violet Alford states that sword dances were evolved by metal workers and that they belong to mining districts and not to agricultural peoples.* I take the opposite view. As I understand the problem, sticks were used by the first agriculturalists, the Sumerians, for if they had had another intent, the ritual dances would not have followed the sun numbers (eight and six) or the moon number (five), neither would they have had the same figures and steps! One cannot put the plough before the horse. It seems logical, therefore, to accept that stick dances created by agricultural people would come first, followed by the stronger, louder implements, the swords, later, when metal came to be worked. Also, there are few sword dances in places that have no mining districts near them. Since swords are connected with mining rituals, districts far from mines would not have sword dances. They would be pointless.

But what preceded the sword dance? *Chain dances* are known to have existed many centuries before metal was discovered. The earliest representation of a chain dance dates back to the 'feather head-dress people' who lived in Egypt in predynastic times. A carving on a rock, north-east of Luxor in upper Egypt, depicts a chain dance of around 3400 BC. Chain dances were ritual dances, performed to protect people, animals or settlements from disease, evil influences and enemies. These were of sacred origin and therefore tended to survive centuries after the motive for their invention ceased to be believed in. The belief that a circle had the magic effect of protection from evil is attested by the enormously wide diffusion of circle formations in all countries. The 'magic circle' is believed in even in our times, and there are dances in Europe where dancers hold hands, hold handerkerchiefs, hold scarves, hold sticks, and of course hold swords, for the link-up between dancers. When metal

*A German folklorist, Richard Wolfram, has tried to prove that all sword dances derived from Germanic sources, but this is an unlikely theory since sword dances are recorded as having been performed in Crete by Kouretes at the birth of Zeus, to prevent his father Kronos from swallowing him up!

hold handerkerchiefs, hold scarves, hold sticks, and of course hold swords, for the link-up between dancers. When metal came into use, to be linked by metal swords was the most powerful magic of all.

It is Violet Alford's belief that the chain dance preceded the sword dance and that at some time swords were introduced into the sacred chain, where previously men had used sticks. She also maintains that hoop dances are alternatives for sword dances, the figures and steps being almost the same in most dances, and identical in others.

The *Trawanteldanz* of Flanders is somewhat different, however, for there long sticks link the dancers in a closed ring. A hoop lies in the centre, and is picked up by one dancer with his sticks (without letting go with either hand). He then passes it over his right arm, up to his head, down around his body, steps over it, picks it up with the left hand and stick, and passes it on to the next man who does the same with the hoop, and so round the ring, no one having let go his two sticks during the whole time! I saw it done, but still do not understand how it is done. The dancers said the hoop represented the sun, and each man was purified by passing through the 'sun'. Note that the hoop went round sunwise: to the left of the ring. This is the only example of this type of dance known to me.

Violet Alford believes that the chain, whether in a ring or in a snaky line, is a symbol of good luck, especially if the ring moves clockwise (sunwise). This is quite logical, and I have never heard this statement denied. A Tibetan monk once told me that a circle moving to the left – sunwise – meant the sun, while if it moved to the right, it represented the moon. This, he said, was the same with a swastika; if it turned sunwise it called for the sun, if it turned to the right it called for the moon.

Hilt-and-point sword dances are a form of chain dance, because each dancer grasps his own sword in his right hand, holding the point of his neighbour's sword in his left hand, thus forming an unbroken chain. Sometimes this chain is straight, sometimes it curves into snake figures, sometimes it makes a closed ring, but it is always an unbroken chain. It has nothing to do with the pyrrhic dance, which is an exercise to train the soldiers or fighting men to be agile and nimble. An example of the pyrrhic dance is practised by some African tribes, where two lines of warriors thrust their lances rhythmically forward at regular distances, while each dancer in turn leaps all along the double row of sharp lances, only escaping the fierce thrusts of his fellows by nimbly jumping aside, while keeping to the rhythm of the dance.

Sword dances exist in Betanzos and accounts have been written about them. The figure of hilt-and-point chain dance occurs in the dances. (Manuel Antonio de Verin, Perez Seixas and Gonzales de Hervia of Betanzos wrote about them in 1886, in *El Librador.*)

There are other examples to be found in Huelva, south-western Spain, and some very complicated ones further north in Burgos, Galicia, Aragón, Extremadura and Cataluña.

Ricardo del Arco, the Spanish folklorist, studied ritual dances in high Aragón (the mountainous regions in north-eastern Spain), and described some of them in his book *Notas de Folklore Altos Aragonés* (Madrid, 1945). One of the dances described is 'El Dance' (in masculine form), which makes it a ritual dance as opposed to 'La Danza' which, being the feminine form, makes it a social dance. He unfortunately describes as 'guerreras' (war dances), the sword dances in Ribagorza and Ainsa, both of which are danced either with swords or sticks. This immediately shows they are agricultural dances. These stick dances are very similar to the Basque sword and stick dances, of course.

Ricardo del Arco also noticed that some English Morris dances were almost exactly similar to the Basque ones and those of his own country, even the costumes worn by the dancers, and some hobby horses carried as in the Province of

Huesca and in Cataluña. He explained this as a Celtic inheritance, although this is unlikely since, as we have seen, in ancient times the priests of Greece, the Near East and Rome performed similar ritual dances 'for full jars'.

The Basque country possessed the Januzi Dantza, which comprises seven jumps. This dance also exists in France and Westphalia.

Christians and Moors battles. Violet Alford considers that the Christians and Moors rituals came about after the defeat of the Moors in the fifteenth century, but the earliest recorded dates are the twelfth century AD and the Moors left Spain in the fifteenth century AD. However, this rite is much older than the Moors in my opinion. It must have been evolved many hundreds of years previously; indeed, they could well be the fights between the Old Year and the New Year, or the fight between Good and Evil, for the Christians are always Good and White, whereas the Moors (or Turks) are always Bad and Black and they invariably lose.

In Aragón spring festivals always contain maypole dances, as well as sword and stick dances in the streets. After numerous recitations about weather, and laudatory rhymes to the patron saint, stereotyped battles take place with swords and four boys called 'angels', who climb on men's shoulders to make a 'castle'.

In Lerida, as in Cataluña and other parts of Spain maypole dances are favourites. The maypole is the tree of life, or the sacred tree, emblem of fertility, venerated for many thousands of years.

The scapegoat. In Provence the scapegoat is called 'le bouc émissaire' and comes out at carnival times. The Old Year is called 'la Vieille Femme' and she is sawn in two (being thought of as the embodiment of winter) to make sure that winter is dead and gone. This custom is also prevalent in Spain, Italy and in other French provinces, says Marcelle Mourgues.

Hobby horses already existed in 600 BC, says J. Troubet. At

Christians and Moors
In the Penedes region (eastern Spain), the Christians and Moors are not represented as Giants, as in other parts of the Peninsula. Two lines of dancers – eight or nine – dance as if riding on horseback, they meet, strike sword against shield, separate, dance round again, meet once more, strike again, and so on – but it is always the Christians who win in the end. Sometimes they ride hobby-horses. At times the Moors do not possess swords, just shields. They represent Evil (the black) against Good (the white), or the New Year fighting off the Old Year.

carnival time in Provence, a 'cheval blanc' comes out and dances in 'Les Belles' and in 'Les Figures', two Provençal dances. Other dances of the region are 'Le Soufflet', 'Les Fileuses', 'La Fricassée' and the 'Folies d'Espagne', which take place on Ash Wednesday, as does 'Le Bouffet'. In Auvergne women are said to roll in the mud to bring forth new vegetation (Frazer).

Devils have many names according to the district. For example, in Galicia, north-west Spain, they are called Gamachina, Fereneiros, Metouro, Gashino. The names are used for devils as well as for Fools (jesters) in sword dances and in mummers' plays. (See Professor Perez' article *Las Antiguas Fiestas de Corpus Christi y de San Roque en Betanzos* (Ancient Festivals of Corpus Christi and of St Roque in Betanzos).)

CHAPTER THREE

More about rituals

LET US TAKE a further look at the origins of some of the rituals and the dances in which they are performed: those to do with rain and fertility are often at the core and are of obvious importance to man.

RAIN

We shall first examine some *rain-enforcing customs* performed by so-called primitive people, such as the Australian aborigines, and those in parts of Asia, south-east Africa, and islands like the Celebes. To control floods and excessive downpours, a young girl would be sent out in the rain with a fire-brand; as water was 'dried up' by fire, so, it was thought, the excess rain would dry up. In some parts, the Arabs throw ashes into the air, to 'absorb' the rain, while puffing and shouting to drive it away. Many such rites are carried out to send dark clouds away and so stop rain from spoiling the crops.

On the other hand special magicians are trained – some for several years – to bring rain. Twigs are dipped in water and sprinkled from trees to ensure rain. Two sticks are rubbed together by a man in a tree, to simulate lightning, precursor of rain. In central Australia magicians make themselves bleed to show the rain that it must fall. In Abyssinia, two villages used to fight fiercely to bring rain – until the emperor Menelik II (1889–1913) forbade the custom. Among the Greeks of Thessaly and Macedonia, when rain failed it used to be customary to send children, led by a girl dressed in leaves and flowers, to all the springs and wells in the neighbourhood; the leader would be drenched by the children, and they would sing to call for rain. The Serbians have similar customs with the girl, the Dodola, asking for rain as they sing. The world is full of such practices among the agriculturalists. In Africa, the Wagogo sacrifice black sheep, black fowls and black cattle at the graves of their ancestors, black symbolising rainclouds darkening the sky. In Samoa a sacred stone was kept till rain was needed, then taken by a procession of priests and dipped in a stream.

Stones are wonderful things: they are thought to do miracles where man fails. In Brittany peasants will dip a cross in water to cause rain. France has several of these sacred sites with miracle-working stones. In Navarre the image of St Peter is dipped in water to ask for rain. (And on the coast, if the catch of fish is disappointing, his image is dipped in the sea as a punishment!) In Mingrelia the Shans drench the image of Buddha to demand rain. In parts of Russia and Japan mock thunder is believed to bring rain for crops. Innumerable practices for the control of rain are registered all over the world.

FERTILITY RITES

In Thuringen (Germany) and in Franche-Compté (France) women leap and jump at carnival time to make the hemp grow tall. (James Frazer, *The Golden Bough*, p.28). They believe that through their sympathetic magic, they will obtain their wish.

In Sumatra rice is sown by women who let their hair hang loose, down their backs, in order that the rice may grow luxuriantly and have long stalks. In ancient Mexico, they had a festival held in honour of the goddess of maize, or 'the long-haired Mother' as they called her. During this festival the women's hair was kept unbound. They shook and tossed it about in the dances which were the chief feature in the ceremonial, so that the maize might be correspondingly luxuriant and 'that the people might have abundance'. In many parts of Europe dancing or leaping high in the air are approved homeopathic modes of making the crops grow high, as is done nowadays still, in our Morris dances and similar ritual dances by men.

The magic virtue of a *pregnant woman* to communicate *fertility* is known to Bavarian and Austrian peasants, who think that if you give a woman with child the first fruit of a tree to eat, the tree will bring forth abundantly the following year. In parts of Europe women will still embrace a tree trunk in order to obtain a child.

The Greeks and Romans sacrificed pregnant victims to the goddesses of the corn and of the earth, doubtless in order that the earth might teem with harvests and the corn swell in the ear. In Europe it is believed that a fruitful woman makes plants fruitful, whereas a barren woman makes them barren. On the other hand, plants could influence man; the Tree of Life is a standard example of this belief.

Certain *stones* were thought to bring fertility to crops and the animal kingdom. The Indians of Peru employed certain stones for the increase of their maize crops, others for the increase of potatoes, and yet others for the increase of livestock. The stones used to make maize grow were fashioned in the likeness of cobs of maize, and the stones designed to multiply flocks had the shape of sheep. Stones, like plants and animals, were thought to possess a soul and therefore could influence humans, just as humans could influence plants and animals.

THE CORN SPIRIT

The concept of the corn spirit as being old and dead at harvest time is very clearly demonstrated in a custom of the Arabs of Moab. In that country, when only a small portion of the field remains to be reaped, the owner takes a handful of wheat tied up in a sheaf. A hole is dug in the form of a grave and two stones are set upright at the head and the foot, just as in a human burial. The sheaf of wheat is laid in the grave and a sheikh pronounces these words: 'The Old Man is dead'. Earth is thrown on the grave with a prayer – 'May Allah bring us back the wheat of the dead'.

In ancient Egypt, at sowing time, the Pharaoh and his Queen came out, together with the priests leading the sacred Bull. After offering it some emmer (primitive wheat), the Pharaoh and his Queen performed fertility rites in the furrows, after which the field was ploughed, and young girls sowed the seed. This ceremony would ensure the growth of the corn, and a good harvest. The priests used to make effigies of the god *Osiris*, made of earth and corn, and bury these figures in the fields, for good crops. If, after the harvest, the effigies were taken up again and the corn was found to have sprouted 'from the body of Osiris' this would be hailed as a good omen for the success of the crops. The corn god 'had died that the people might live'.

Some legends from Norway, and the Fly River in Papua New Guinea, tell of a belief that if the ruler or priest was cut into pieces after death and the pieces buried in different fields, those fields would bring forth good harvests.

The god *Osiris* was a tree spirit as well as an earth spirit, and as such was responsible for the fruitfulness of trees, including the pine tree and the 'eriea-tree' (the oak). Osiris' worshippers were forbidden to injure fruit trees. He is also connected with grape-vines – according to a papyrus of 1550 BC, in which he is represented as sitting in a shrine surrounded by clusters of grapes. Osiris was certainly a god of vegetation and fertility, as descriptions of his festivals confirm.

Isis was the goddess of cereals, according to Diodorus Seculus. Wheat and barley were her responsibility and their discovery was attributed to her. The Greeks conceived Isis as a corn goddess, for they identified her with *Demeter*. Amongst many other names she is called the 'corn mother', the 'mother of the ears of corn'. She was represented in figurines as having ears of corn on her head, or in her hand. According to some historians the worship of Isis was brought over from Egypt to the northern Mediterranean coasts. The Greeks believed that Demeter was the Goddess Earth; others believed she was the Goddess of the Corn. There seems to be some controversy here. It is understandable that since early man noticed that only female creatures brought forth new life, the earth must be feminine since grass, trees and plants were born from her. She was thought therefore to be the goddess of vegetation. Her daughter Persephone ultimately came to represent the regeneration of nature – spring. Both goddesses were connected with corn. In *The Golden Bough* (p.397), Frazer states that Demeter was believed in as 'goddess of the corn among the Christians' descendants in Greece, at her sanctuary of Eleusis' down to the nineteenth century AD. Dodwell visited Eleusis in the nineteenth century and saw the statue of Demeter in the centre of a threshing floor, amongst the ruins of a temple. The inhabitants lamented the loss of their statue – said to be now in the University of Cambridge. In *The Gate of Horn*, Gertrude Levy illustrates reliefs from ancient Greece, in which Demeter (the matron), Persephone (the maid) and Apollo (the sun god) were represented. 'Without the help of the young god there would be no new spring' – and no good harvests. Hence it seems reasonable to assume that the numerous folk dances all over Europe for two women and one man, were a representation of this trio. Early man danced his aims and his ambitions to ensure, through sympathetic magic, food for the community and good luck.

In some parts of the eastern Mediterranean and central Europe, Demeter was called the Corn Mother, but according to the crop, she may be called the Pea Mother, the Rye Mother, or the Barley Mother as well. In parts of Magdeburg

(Germany) it is sometimes said, 'It will be a good year for flax, for the Flax Mother has been seen'. In Britain the Corn Mother, or Corn Dolly, is still made up from straw from the last sheaf cut in the field. The spirit of the corn is said to be kept in her image till the following year. Many parts of Europe have kept up customs relating to the corn mother. At times she is feared in case she gets cross and refuses to let the corn grow, but mostly she is venerated because she brings forth the new crops. In some parts of Europe the last sheaf is hung in the barn till the following spring, then taken to the fields for good luck. Many different rites are kept up in various parts of Europe. In France the last sheaf is made into a puppet dressed in blue and white, a branch of a tree is stuck in her breast, and she is then called 'Ceres'. In East Prussia, at the wheat or rye harvest, the woman who reaps the last sheaf is told, 'You are getting the Old Grandmother'. Whoever gets this sheaf will marry in the next year. A similar belief exists in Ireland. Each district in all European countries has different rites associated with the last sheaf of corn gathered from the fields, all of them with the intention of good harvests or continuity in the harvests from year to year. Even the animals on the farm are thought to profit from participation in the last sheaf! Dancing is often part of the ceremonies. Sometimes the ancient Greek belief in Demeter and Persephone is found in the double female dolls, or puppets, called the 'Old Woman and the Maid.' Or in some parts a male and a female impersonator will act to ensure good harvests the following year.

Just as the spirit of spring may be represented by a tree and by a person, so the spirit of the corn, or harvest, may be shown in the last sheaf, or by the person who cut it. In America it is the maize mother who presides over good harvests; in the East Indies, it is the rice mother. In Peru the best of the maize plants was dressed as a female puppet and worshipped. In Malaya the rice is said to have a soul which has to be coaxed into a basket before the rice is cut – so that it does not escape. During the flowering of the rice, noise near the fields is avoided, and blasphemous words are not spoken, for fear the plants might be offended. There are as many variants in the ceremonies in the East as there are in Europe, all with the object of ensuring greater crops and the preservation of the corn spirit for the following year. In some cases the new seed is treated as a newborn child, while the farmer's wife has to follow the rules prescribed for a woman who has just given birth. In some cases two puppets are made up of rice ears and called Rice Bride and Rice Bridegroom, and are placed in a part of the barn called the bridal chamber.

HUMAN SACRIFICES

Human sacrifices were common in South America to promote crops; in Ecuador, for instance, one hundred children were killed at sowing time. The ancient Mexicans also had child sacrifices for their maize crops. The Pawnees sacrificed a teenage girl, cut her body into small pieces and placed them in the fields. A West African queen sacrificed a man and a women for the same purpose. It appears that most of the Philippine Islands included human sacrifices in their sowing practices, as did parts of India such as the Brahmaputra, part of Bengal, and among the Khonds. Early man believed that the corn spirit was impersonated by a human being, who, like the corn, had to be propitiated in spring and killed in autumn (some tribes killed the corn spirit in spring and buried pieces of the 'spirit' in the fields to make it fertile, as we have seen). Later, instead of humans, animals were used to impersonate the corn spirit. In Britain and Germany it was the dog and the wolf; other animals were the hare, the cock, the bull or cow, the pig, or the bear. One can understand the bear easily, for this clever creature knew when winter was coming, hibernating in a cave during the cold months, only coming out at the approach of spring; therefore he became an emblem of spring, of the regeneration of nature. The famous bear dances enacted in the Pyrenees symbolised the coming of spring. For some strange reason, in Germany, Switzerland and the Isle of Skye and parts of France a cat and a goat were also considered to incarnate the corn spirit; the horse, in parts of Britain. Some birds are also thought to represent the spirit of the corn and to bring forth good harvests.

If we turn to China, there is an ancient tradition that on the first day of spring – at the beginning of the Chinese New Year, often in February – the prefect or governor of the city goes to the east gate and sacrifices to the 'Divine Husbandman', represented by a man with a bull's head. This recalls the worship of Mithras – the bull religion. This ancient ox, or bull, was filled with corn. This rite seems akin to the Athenian *Bouphonia,* bull sacrifice.

THE SUN

The sun, too, was thought to be a charm against evil – a way of protecting plants, animals and man from diseases, a method of promoting fertility in nature and a means of purification as well. Hence the world-wide custom of lighting bonfires, throwing lighted discs in the air and twirling huge lighted wheels on poles to emulate the sun at certain times of the year like midsummer, midwinter, spring and autumn.

For example, the ancient Egyptians thought that if the Pharaoh walked round a temple during an eclipse, the sun would come back, for walking round would sustain the sun during the eclipse. Most peoples evolved magic rites to enable the sun to come and ripen harvests, light up the sky, create growth in nature. Examples are innumerable and include dances by priests or holy men imitating the sun's cycle in the sky by forming a circle in the dance. The sun being good luck for the crops, most folk dances start by moving 'sunwise' – like the hands of a clock. The ancient

STILT DANCER
The Anguiano stilt dancer in his yellow skirt represents the sun. He and his seven companions must turn constantly to show the sun what to do. He wears stilts because he is a deity and must be taller than humans. The multi-coloured ribbons of his jacket are reminiscent of some English Morris teams. He carries castanets.

Mexicans used to catch victims from neighbouring tribes, and tear their hearts out of their breast, to offer to the sun 'and give it strength'. The ancient Greeks believed the sun rode in a chariot drawn by four horses. In Rhodes each year, a chariot and four horses were thrown into the sea for the sun to ride in the sky next day; Rhodes was not alone in sacrificing horses to the sun.

The sun's beneficent influence over nature was encouraged, too, by bonfires lit at certain times of the year with the specific aim of emulating and honouring the sun.

In our day on midsummer's eve, bonfires are lit and effigies burnt in certain towns, as in the 'Fallas' of Valencia, where the main streets are lit up by bonfires on which several life-sized puppets in gorgeous clothes are burnt. Prizes are given to the best figures, round the fires. Historical figures are represented, or local dignitaries; even Charlie Chaplin has figured amongst them. A jury chooses the prizewinners. Everyone in a particular street contributes during the year to the expense of these figures, which are really fantastic.

This festival and others similar in intent record the ancient custom of sacrificing humans and animals to the sun deity, to give it strength and ensure that it returns the following year. Numerous instances of these bonfires are recorded in various parts of Europe. In Luchon, France, live serpents were burnt, and in Paris live cats, said to incarnate witches, up to the last century. It is said that the Celts preserved these customs longest in Europe. According to W. Mannhardt the burning of humans and animals promoted fertility by securing the sunshine needed for crops. On the other hand, some authorities believe that the burning of humans and animals simulates the destruction of witches, the bringers of evil. It is difficult to determine which of the two theories is correct.

SOME EXAMPLES OF RITUAL DANCES

Ricardo del Arco describes festivals for shepherds and their flocks, before they go off to the mountains for summer pastures, where they remain several months. These festivals are called *Pastoradas* and in many of them the *Christians and Moors mummers* take part, as well as the Chief Shepherd, his Deputy (the Rapatan), the Guardian Angel, often the Devil or Lucifer too; in many villages the 'Danzantes' (ritual men dancers) take part. Lengthy recitations are delivered – mainly on Christianity, the weather and any special village news or gossip.

For example in Ainsa (Zaragoza region) the 'Moorish' and 'Christian' contingents meet, attend the religious festival in church, then fight – the Christians always winning, of course, since they represent good, as opposed to the Moorish (black) evil. For New Year, these two factions often come out to pacify the region before the coming New Year – which must start clean and white. After their defeat the Moors must always be converted to Christianity. The Church permitted these customs since it could not eradicate them, and everyone is happy with the compromise. After a ritual dance (like an English Morris dance), the Chief Shepherd delivers his recitation – all of which takes up to three hours! After some general singing, a ritual dance is performed once more and a religious procession takes place. After a lengthy meal, a public dance is held in the village square. At times, the Devil and the Archangel have altercations, but the Angel always wins. The Moors and Christians may fight several times, but by the end of the night the Moorish King has his head cut off (in mimicry, of course).

The priests traditionally write out the recitations of the various characters since until 1936 most peasants could not read or write and, of course, the festivals have been taking place for many centuries.

In Torres del Obispo, 'La Morisca' (the fight between Moors and Christians) used only to take place after a good harvest – about every ten years – but nowadays it is performed more frequently. In this version, the Moors have three castles into which they retreat before the Christian hosts. After the usual parleys, the Chief Shepherd and his Rapatan discuss events, a religious procession is formed and the Christian hosts demand large sums of money from the

Moors, whose castle is being burnt! The Devil has a part in this, but he finally flees before the intense heat and shower of fireworks.

At Salrinana and at Sena, the procession comprises 'Charles the Great' led by bagpipers and shawm players. This starts before daybreak, and ritual dancers perform all the way to church. They then fetch the Mayor and the Church Council, dancing all the time, with or without sticks, according to the dance. They reserve their sword dance for the main square. The Moors take the stage and parleys ensue, after which the dancers form a circle, the swords making a platform on to which climb four Angels, called 'Volantes'. After further dances and parleys between the Shepherd and his Rapatan, the Guardian Angel and the Moorish King (instead of the Devil this time), peace is established and all are happy.

Robles, Lavaja, Castejón de Monegos, Almudebar, Capella, Anciles, and innumerable other towns and villages in high Aragón, have each their own version of this festival. Some are held at midsummer, others in spring or autumn, but the theme is the same: Christians and Moors fight, ritual dancing (Morris style) persists, in between Christian religious celebrations. In some villages the Chief Shepherd chooses his shepherdess, who presents him with a *huge* tart. A poplar or a pine tree is cut down and planted in the main square, dances are performed for the patron saint, and the festival ends with a lavish banquet. Some villages add public dancing in the main square. Sword and stick dances are never omitted, while in some places a maypole is erected, to which flowers, or a live cock, are tied, while races are run for the tree prizes.

In some places a 'ronda' is organised: a choir goes round the village singing in front of the houses of important inhabitants, the church, the authorities and young girls of their choice.

At Tolva the 'Pastorada' lasts three days, the gist of the festival being as always 'Grant us good harvests and plentiful herds'. Ritual dances never fail and Christians and Moors play their part, too.

At Yebra there are special celebrations for the festival of Santa Orosia, the martyred saint. After morning Mass, in the square, the head of the saint is uncovered for all to see. There are several dozen of these cloths to be removed and when the head finally emerges, the crowd sighs with relief and joy, all fall on their knees, and the sick who have come to be cured give way to hysterical fits, jerks and cries. Dancing takes place as usual, and the processions go back to the church, the ritual recurring in the afternoon with recitations. Jaca also has a similar festival, only there it is the *body* of the saint, not her head, that performs the miracles.

In Huesca (also in Aragón), on 10th August, ritual dancers take part in a 'Moxiganga' (or 'Mojiganga'). In this folk drama the procession comprises a 'Tarasca' (dragon), a witch, a fool, hobby-horses, bullfights, a maypole dance and the Christians and Moors fight. And, as noted by Strabo, writing on dances of the Spaniards: 'Jotas are the last in a Festival'. Sword and stick dances never fail.

Since we are in the northern provinces, a word must be added to assure those interested that similar festivals exist in Cantabria, Asturias, Galicia and León as well, for all those places unspoilt by tourists have preserved their customs. An interesting one takes place at New Year, that of men wearing sheepskin jackets and a pointed hat, with large cowbells attached to their backs and waists, so that as they walk along the street in groups, their peculiar walk causes the bells to clang furiously, thus driving away all 'evil spirits', and purifying the neighbourhood from all evil before the New Year.

The Basques have a dance with the Fool wearing the double-faced mask – an old black devil in front and a young white man on the back of his mask (Janus and Vesta, or the Old and New Year). This special ritual dance takes place at Ochagavía, where the festival of Our Lady of the Dew is celebrated with special dances in the main square, on top of the sacred hill, and before the sacred ancient oak (reputed to be one thousand years old), a little way down the hill. The dancers perform for it specially, after which they accompany the 'authorities' back to their homes, the last being the Mayor, who regales them with wine and cakes. And the dancers deserve them, for they have danced for half an hour, hardly taking breath.

RITUAL FOLK DRAMAS AND MUMMERS' PLAYS

There are many kinds of mummers' plays and folk dramas, but we shall first look at *Giants and Dwarfs*.

Giants always come out together with dwarfs, who precede them during processions. The origins of giants and dwarfs are not clear, but having read A.B. Cook's book *Zeus* I am convinced that he is right and that giants originated in Sumerian times as deities who protected the cultivation of grain, and promoted its growth. The Sumerians constructed effigies of their vegetation gods, and carried them on floats from field to field, so that the crops might be blessed; and from shrine to shrine, so that the deities could visit one another and thus promote good relationships. Being gods required them to be taller than human beings – just as up to the last century painters represented the saints and Christ as taller than the rest of humanity, since they were more important than ordinary humans. As Neolithic man went westwards into Europe in search of more land to cultivate, so he brought with him his knowledge of the rituals to protect the crops, and thus encourage their growth. So in the Iberian Peninsula, Italy, parts of Greece and Belgium giants are carried about and venerated. I should say here that it seems that the Belgian giants were taken to that country by the Spanish troops of Charles the Great, who made himself king of the Netherlands, and later by those of Charles V.

Giants
These two giants are the white queen and king, meaning Good, the New Year and Christianity. The 'window' half way down the skirt is for the carrier to breathe through. Giants can be up to eighteen feet high and quite a weight (heavy osier frame).

To go back to the *giants* in the Iberian Peninsula, these always go in pairs: a White King and Queen (good, or the New Year), and the Black King and Queen (evil, or the Old Year), representing the male and female principles and creating a 'perfect' entity. Since, as far as the performers are concerned, the origin of the giants is lost in antiquity, it has been thought proper to add a Red King and Queen (North American Indians) and a Yellow King and Queen (China and Japan), thus representing the whole of humanity. The total number of giants is thus eight. Some richer cities like Burgos and Tarragona have two semi-giants as well, a peasant couple dressed in the costumes of the peasants of the region. These are larger than the dwarfs, but not so important as the giants. Some giants are carried by strong fellows, so they can dance, as in Avila, Burgos and some other big cities, but it requires strength to carry an 18-foot figure of osier, dressed in velvets, satins, damask silks, carrying a sword or sceptre, a scimitar, a large papier-mâché head with a turban or a heavy metal crown and often a cloak to boot. Yet the carrier can dance a 'jota', which is a lively dance!

The fact that there is a king and a queen appears to derive from the belief of early man in the duality of life. He noticed that there had to be two sides to every question: an active (male) and a passive (female) side. The duality was to be observed everywhere, for example, in heat and cold, summer and winter, day and night, etc., and without both male and female aspects there would be no new life. Early man therefore evolved the androgyne (a man/woman), who embodied both principles in a perfect whole. Hence the giants have both a king and a queen.

When a giant carrier wants a rest, he leaves the figure on its four cane legs and goes off. Parents of small children, meanwhile, bring their offspring to the giant to shake hands; for good luck, they say. These giants are often housed in the cathedral or the town hall when not on duty, as in Tarragona, Burgos, Santiago de Compostela, etc; the local

Morris men (ritual dancers) also dance in the cathedral or in churches, as in Sevilla, Santo Domingo de Silos, and many other towns in Cantabria and the North. Giants in the Peninsula do not seem to have been connected with mountains, seas and sky, or to have preceded the gods, as they do in Scandinavia.

Dwarfs are of normal height, being people (men) wearing papier mâché heads at least two feet tall, making their bodies look stunted. They represent the notables and groups of people who make up the community: the mayor, lady mayoress, midwife, doctor, night-watchman, baby, nurse, a peasant and his wife, a fisherman, his wife, the schoolmaster, etc. All this nowadays, but originally they represented the spirits of the underworld, the 'little people', in charge of making the pastures and seeds grow. Dwarfs in large cities number up to sixteen, to make four squares of four dancers each – a lucky number. There must always be not less than eight dwarfs, for eight is a lucky number meaning 'eternity', or world without end. Morris teams employ the figure of eight very frequently, just as they do in other parts of Europe and Asia. The dwarfs are accompanied by shawm and drum, the traditional instruments. The shawm is sometimes called 'gaita' (an Arabic word), and in some parts it is called a 'dulzaina'. In Galicia and the Northwest the bagpipe and drum are the usual instruments.

These figures are most impressive. Dwarfs represent a vital factor in an agricultural community – the spirits of the underworld – and their duty was to cause the seed to sprout and pastures to flourish. During animistic pagan times all vegetation, stones and animals had their own soul or spirit, and the little people of the underworld (fairies to us) were of the greatest importance to man and to nature. In some cases the little people were deemed to work metal, or to guard mines. It was said that staircases existed in trunks of old trees for them to go up and down to and from the underworld.

Unfortunately, in a poor locality like San Pedro Manrique

Dwarfs
Dwarfs, who always process in front of the Giants, represent the spirits of the underworld, who are responsible for the growth of crops and pastures. They can look many different characters, but always with an enormous papier-mâché head.

(Logroño, Castile), the giants and dwarfs are left to be taken round by boys, because the men cannot be paid a fee. Hence the figures are not well looked after. This is a great pity, for thus the old traditions will be forgotten.

Giants do not perform special figures in their dance, they just outline some steps individually, whereas dwarfs perform figures like the cross, circle (clockwise for the sun figures, anticlockwise for the moon), the half-moon or crescent, cast off (like the ram's horns), figures of eight, etc, for the aims in their dances were similar to those of ritual dancers.

It has been suggested that the 'fight' between Christians and Moors, as shown nowadays, represents the expulsion of the Moors from Spain in the fifteenth century. The Moors invaded Spain in 711 AD, but we may be certain that many ritual observances were in existence thousands of years before the Moors ever thought of coming into Europe. That they left many traces of their 700 years' stay in the Peninsula is certain, but rites connected with the promotion of crops date far back, before 711 AD!

The reason why this fight is now called 'Christians and Moors' is probably a question of fashion. When the Moors were expelled from Spain, it became the fashion to wear Turkish turbans and wide trousers, veils and some items of Arab clothing among the aristocracy – as portraits in stately homes will show us. It became the fashion, also, to call some dances 'Morisca', 'Moresca', 'Mauresque' (in France) and 'Moriscada'. As the Turks had been harrassing the northern coast of the Mediterranean for some three hundred years, they were considered as the evil-doers as against the Christians – the goodies. So in the Peninsula, seasonal ritual dramas became the fashion, but now dressing the contestants as Moors/Turks versus Christians. These fights are enacted at Corpus Christi, or midsummer, or in some places at Easter. Some of the Fools in ritual dance teams in Spain wear masks with an old, ugly face in front and a young, handsome one at the back, such as is worn by the Fool at Ochagavía: an indication of the origin of this dance in the fight between the Old and New Years.

It should be remembered that ritual dancers impersonated spirits (and many of them in primitive societies today still 'live' their role of spirits, be they good or bad). They had/have to have masks so that their neighbours would not recognise them, and the easiest way to make a mask is to paint one's face black, or at least paint it in a striking way, which is different from everyday use. On this subject James Frazer said: 'Village customs to blacken one's face were not because the dancers were thought to represent Moors, but rather that the dancers were thought to represent Moors because their faces were blackened'.

In Cataluña the fight takes the form of two snaky lines of men on hobby-horses, one line dressed as Turks, or Moors, the other as Christians. The Moors usually wear richer costumes than the Christians and carry scimitars, or metal or wooden swords and shields. In some villages the Moors carry a shield only, as they can only defend themselves and can never win. As the snaky lines meander in opposite directions, they curve back towards each other; and every time they meet, Christians and Moors clash swords – or swords on shields – and move on, to meet again and again.

In some larger towns the two factions dress richly in silks, velvets and gold braid, showing off their civic wealth. Villena, north of Alicante, is one of those fortunate places, where a pageant takes place yearly and lasts a whole week, prizes being distributed at the end of the week. Each group is preceded by a band of musicians. It is a glorious sight that lasts the morning, the afternoon, the evening, of the first day, and they continue next day – a little tired, perhaps, but still the feast goes on for a week. Only the sick, the old and the small children go to bed. The Moors dress more richly than the Christians, therefore many people prefer to be Moors. They have adopted a special way of marching to show off the width of their satin trousers, by swishing the leg out and round at every step. Some of the Christian groups are 'pirates' and go about with a black patch over the eye. Some are 'students' in black velvet suits, each carrying an enormous wooden spoon to show they are perpetually hungry. Some riders perform on their lovely arab horses, who dance and bow to order and gallop up and down to the sounds of a band. Their riders are gorgeously dressed as Moors. Each group has a captain who struts about showing off his sword, and he looks up at the balconies filled with spectators who shower cigars down upon the little band to show their appreciation of both performance and turn-out.

So that the girls should not be left out of the show, lorry-loads of young ladies decked out in Moorish clothes sit in the highly decorated and flower-bedecked conveyances. They all look like oriental princesses. Each lorry of people has a store of sweets, which they distribute to the crowd as they pass. This custom evolved from the time when in ancient Greece and Rome (perhaps earlier?) seeds were strewn about in the streets for the crowd as a good luck sign. Traces of this custom still survive in Valencia, where rice is thrown, in Lisbon, where maize is thrown to the crowds, and in Nice, where plaster pellets are thrown round onto the crowds, who, knowing what will happen, carry special umbrellas to avoid being pelted with the beastly things! But in Villena, one boy collected so many sweets he had about six pounds from the afternoon procession – let alone the evening one.

At dusk, when processions retire for refreshments, ancient blunderbusses are loosed off. Clouds of abominable stench waft about and the noise, aimed at driving away evil spirits so that the New Year would be trouble-free, is insupportable. Dogs, adults and children flee from this exercise!

The evening procession is a marvel of decorated coaches with heavily caparisoned mules and horses, their embellishments being of unbelievable wealth and colour. The young ladies adorn these coaches like glamorous flowers. Most people never go to bed, but next morning are ready for the procession almost at daybreak. How do they do it?

Some peasants from the rice fields of the plains also process, dressed mainly in green satin breeches, short jackets and frilly shirts, and carrying gorgeous blankets, which are not known among the peasantry in Spain. Others wear dark breeches and jacket, waistcoats heavily embroidered with silken flowers all over the front, and a cocked hat. Some mariners wear wide, white pleated knickers that look like kilts, Greek fashion. This is not surprising, since the Greeks founded colonies along this coast.

In some towns like Alcoy, further south, this festival of 'Christians and Moors' is equally brilliant, but the merry-makers ride in 'Roman chariots' and wear long flowing cloaks – most alluring. Their festival lasts a week also. Rodney Gallop in his book on Portugal describes a wonderful festival of Christians and Moors in Soubrado, in the northern provinces of Portugal, where a whole day is devoted to the fight, and many characters take part on a kind of stage. Since the Moors never reached northern Portugal, this festival, or ritual fight, must either have been imported from much further south, or must be an indigenous successor of the archaic belief in the fight between the Old Year and the New Year, mentioned earlier. This festival is so much part of the yearly events throughout the Peninsula that one is convinced of its 'home-grown' ancestry.

In some places a castle was built every year, and a Princess was installed to be fought over by the contesting forces. The Christians always won, of course; the Moors were converted to Christianity and the Princess was saved.

With the advent of Christianity, the Christians took over from the New Year (and Good as well as Purity), while the part of the Old Year with all its evils was assigned to the Moors, the Black Ones. Every town and village has its own version of the fight between the two opposites. Nowadays the origin of the opposing forces has been forgotten, so in such places as Villena a most imposing week-long festival takes place – as we have seen – but never a hint of a fight.

RITUAL QUARRELS IN FOLK DANCE

Some dances contain a strange figure, during which partners seem to quarrel, but soon 'make it up' and continue to dance most happily.

One example is the 'Zángano' (getting cross) which occurs in several dances of the province of León, during which the partners suddenly come together and bump each other sideways with the hip, look astonished at each other, laugh, and then continue to dance, smiling happily. At this point the music and step quickens, and the dance changes theme: they go off together triumphantly! Another instance occurs in the 'Jota Valencia', when, during the dance, partners step away from each other, performing a zig-zag step. They describe a triangle, and suddenly come together with a bump! They look crossly at one another, then laugh and alter the step and figure to a jolly tune, describing a 'V' pattern on the ground. Another example is in the 'Tanguillo', where a lot of footwork (zapateado) takes place. At one point partners – who have been performing the same steps – turn to each other and the man stamps a rhythm very crossly, while the woman remains stationary. Then she stamps the same rhythm crossly while he remains still. Then they change steps and perform the same steps once more to a soft music, while they look at each other, performing graceful steps together. Their quarrel is over! It appears to be a representation of what may occur in married life: differences of opinion may take place but reconciliation is always possible! Another example is from Burgos. After coming forward together, partners stop progressing, and she turns round, under his arm. Then he turns round. These two turns are repeated. Then they decide to join both hands, and both turn together, not one after the other as at first. This reconciles them, so music and steps change completely, and both make hops to right then to left, swinging the leg in a jolly, quick tempo, till the music stops, when she suddenly turns under his arm, to bow to him, a bow which he, of course, returns.

CHAPTER FOUR

Notes on style, movement and regional variations

IN THIS CHAPTER I have gathered all sorts of points, tips, rules and interesting background information to help maintain the accuracy and informed authenticity of folk dancing now.

Of course, there is no objection to inventing a dance, but for heaven's sake, don't call these inventions folk dances – say frankly 'invented by so-and-so'!

But my interest will always be in genuine folk dance, danced properly. Usually there is a reason for the particular way a step is performed and it is worth knowing, because if you do not know, you may be apt to modify the movement and thus lose the meaning completely. So I include here a few such explanations to help dancers to keep the traditional style of movements and steps in Spanish folk dances.

STYLE AND MOVEMENT AND THEIR SOURCES

In some steps the girls have to swish their *skirts* round, with the help of the leg, forward and outward; and flick the toe with a quick out-in movement performed with a slightly bent knee. This is in order to show the petticoat for an instant only, and so enable prospective mothers-in-law to see whether the petticoat has a hand-made lace frill and ribbons threaded through round the petticoat. There is just enough time to see this as the bent leg swishes round. The reason for this is that if a girl's father is sufficiently well-to-do, he will hire hands to help him in the fields or on the farm; if he has not enough money to pay workmen, the children have to help in the fields, so the girls would not have time to sit at home and make lace or embroidery work. If crops fail, or some other catastrophe occurs, unless the father has some reserves to fall back upon, the fate of the family would be tragic. So prudent mothers would use this way of reassuring themselves about the means of a girl's family!

Dancers who do not know the reason why a knee is raised will either not bother to raise the knee, or will exaggerate and raise the whole leg in a straight line, waist high. This would never do, for a girl should never show her knees immodestly.

In some dances, like the 'Sevillanas' of Andalucia, the toe gives a quick flick when the leg is raised for the fifth movement before placing the foot behind the supporting foot. The reason for this flick is the same as for the swish round of the leg. There is also the 'Destaque' (stand-outer) step from one side to the other, when the body makes half a turn at each step, and the leg in the air is bent, while the toe gives a quick vertical turn before landing a half turn the other way. Otherwise girls should never show their knees!

In the *Sevillana* step, the left foot *must* advance diagonally forward (not just a little forward in front of the right foot) (1), then you must bring the right toe to touch the left heel (2). Take right foot back to original place (3); bring left foot to touch right toe (4); raise left knee diagonally and flick left toe to the left, forward-and-back in a quick movement (5), then bring left foot behind right heel (6). These six movements consist of two bars of three beats each. Then start again, beginning to the right with the right foot. As your partner is opposite you and fairly close, and you each perform the same steps, together you perform, or draw, a lozenge on the ground. This is a feminine symbol of creation, or birth, intended for promoting fertility. What stage-arranged dancers usually do is move the right foot slightly forward in front of the left foot, and step back, hardly making any movement; the swinging slightly forwards and backwards means nothing at all. The purpose and meaning of the step is therefore nullified and lost.

Most real folk dances start *towards the left.* Why? Because going to the left follows the movement of the sun in the sky (like the hands of a clock) and the sun must be reminded by man through sympathetic magic to do its 'duty' of ripening crops and bringing fertility to nature. Traditional dancers start by placing the left foot in or touching the instep of the right foot, so going to the left (sunwise) is easy. Dancers not knowing the significance of starting to the left, automatically start with the right foot to the right, and so obliterate all the meaning of the dance. The sun brings good luck, so one must start to the left.

The arms in most Mediterranean folk dances should be held forward, curved, above the head, to emulate the crescent moon (emblem of birth, new life and rain) and also the horns of the sacred bull god. Some dancers, not knowing the significance of the position of the arms, hold them either at their sides in a W-shaped line, or low down at hip level; if they do hold their arms up, they bend the elbows so much that in no way do they represent a crescent, or the horns of a bull!

In Andalucia, southern Spain, the arms are held differently from the crescent shape. This came about through *Moorish influence*, brought from Persia many centuries ago. In those countries the arms are considered to have genders – the right, active arm is masculine and the left, passive arm is feminine, thus making a 'complete' figure. For each side must have its opposite to make a 'whole' or complete statement. Both arms start above the head, slightly forward, the left shoulder a little in front. The left arm starts its circle by jerking the wrist down (fingers curved), in an outward, downward movement, round to the right across the body and up again to the level of the right arm and hand. Thus a complete circle is created. (As the arm comes up it must be quite close to the body, not away from it.) Then the right arm and wrist do likewise, the right shoulder being slightly forward as the arm goes outward on its circular movement. The wrists must never hide the face. Thus by comprising opposites, each object is comprehensive – so thought early man. If a complete circle is not achieved by each arm, then the 'motive' of the circle is not achieved. Some people are too lazy, or ignorant of the meanings of these movements, to do more than a 'make-believe' slight gesture with each arm, accomplishing nothing – in which case there is no point in making any arm movements.

In Cataluña, north-eastern Spain, where several Greek colonies were founded along the coast for trading purposes, considerable influence from *ancient Greece* still manifests itself. One of the inherited peculiarities kept up since those early times is the way the arms are held in folk dances. They are held shoulder high, curved, and move horizontally, the wrists facing in the same direction, and jerked simultaneously round in a circular motion. They move from left to right, the wrists marking time to the rhythm of the dance. When they are as far right as convenient for comfort, they go slowly from right back to left, the wrists jerking round the opposite way, in a similar circular motion to mark time. The fingers must be bent inwards, the two middle ones more so than the others. This gives the impression of birds flying, and the gestures are reminiscent of doves, the bird of the Goddess of Love, Aphrodite/Venus, and influenced, no doubt, by the Greek colonists who worshipped the Bird Askos or Soul. People who do not bother to conform to the traditional style just flick the hands from time to time, with arms about waist high, so the purpose of the finger and arm position is completely lost.

When crossing over with partner to the opposite place, each dancer should describe a semi-circle to the partner's place, and not walk in a straight line. The purpose of crossing over is to make a half-moon: 'media-luna', the figure is called. The moon being a deity is thus represented in the dance. A *straight* line to the opposite place is just a meaningless figure. Stage-arranged dances are frequently placed in a straight line facing the spectators. This is completely contrary to folk dance tradition, for a folk dance always has a purpose, and entertaining the spectators is *not* one of the aims of a folk dance. The artificial smiles worn by stage dancers are also contrary to tradition. When you have a partner it is to make friends or to see a friend again, for life in ancient times prevented people from meeting often, as each person was occupied with his/her work. Community and courting dances were evolved to enable people to meet friends, and to make new friends. Partners should look at one another, not look at the floor or the heavens! One's partner is not there. . .

Waving to spectators is another item which was invented by stage managers and is contrary to folk dance tradition. Therapeutic dances were performed by medicine-men; young men's war dances were designed to make young men agile, obedient and dexterous, because they had to hunt and to defend the tribe; children's dances were created to teach them the routines of daily life; ritual dancers performed sympathetic magic to promote fertility and ensure *food* for the community; none were created to make an impression on the public.

There is a gesture in some dances that means 'come to me', as an *invitation*. The dancer moves backwards sharply, usually diagonally, onto one foot, while raising a hand (or both hands) forward a little above the head, the middle finger curving downwards, with a graceful sharp movement of the wrist and flexing of the elbow, during the two or three beats. Then there is a sudden step back at right angles, with a brisk 'call' – beckoning with both hands that come down and back behind the body sharply and imperatively. It can also be performed with one hand only; this is a graceful movement of a flexed elbow and wrist, as the dancer moves backwards, ending in a sharp order as the hand twists round, down and back behind the body. Other movements say 'I give you' – both hands shoulder level, giving a twist of the wrists inwards, downwards, upwards and suddenly out towards someone.

When a *hat* is used in a dance it should be held by the brim between finger and thumb, the crown facing the audience and the inside turned towards the dancer. This rule always applies, except at the very end of the dance when the man holds the hat horizontally over the head of his partner as if he were going to put it on her head. This means 'I have got you', or 'You are mine now', for a hat is a sexual symbol. But on no account must the hat be carried horizontally during a dance. If a girl dances with a hat she must look at it as she dances, to attract the attention of the spectators to the hat. These Cordobese hats are either black or grey.

When dancing one hand may be held behind the body while the other is held curved in front of the body, but in *flamenco* dances, both hands must twist the wrists round together as much as possible, and not move only one hand round while the other is hanging motionless to the side. At no time must the hands touch the back of the dancer, though they may be placed on the hips, the back of the hands touching the body at the waist, or one hand at the waist, the other a little lower down. The man may have one hand behind his waist (not touching) while the other is held bent in front of the body. At times in flamenco dances one arm may be going round, down, and up across the front of the body, making a complete circle, while the other arm stays above and a little behind the body (both arms always a little curved, of course). The wrists should be twisting round, the fingers moving separately one after the other, in a circular movement. When both hands are above and a little in front of the head, the other arm comes round in a circle, wrists and fingers working. It should always be remembered that the arm comes down over the 'working foot', that is, if the right foot is forward, the right arm should come down over it, and vice versa. Also, one hand may be moving down and round – outwards – while the other moves upward, or one hand may cross in front of the other to express a determined intention, such as to end a certain movement. The palms of the hands in such a case should be uppermost and the fingers separated and slightly curved inwards.

When holding the skirt, for example, it should be between finger and thumb, the wrists forward and supple, the other fingers open in a fan-shape, and *never* with a closed fist as if the dancer were cold or cross! The shoulders should be held down and back as much as possible, and the back should be arched, but the stomach should never be allowed to push forwards. On the contrary, the position should be similar to that of a bullfighter. His stance in a bullfight was the origin of the flamenco posture. This influence came from the Minoans when they were masters of the Mediterranean and ardent worshippers of the Bull God, whom they sacrificed every year. Before killing it they 'played' it and danced ritual dances around it, enticing it to come and attack the dancers. They climbed on its back and turned somersaults over its head, finally killing it to preserve the strength of the herd. Or so they believed.

The figures painted on the Hagia Triada sarcophagus are interesting. They all carry themselves in a way peculiar to Crete, that is, with a very hollow back, shoulders held back, the bust thrust forward. This pose is most striking. The 'Lily Prince' frescoes, the 'Rhyton-bearers' on other mural paintings, the priestesses and the so-called 'ladies of the court' represented on murals, all have this remarkable posture seen only, in ancient or modern times, in Minoan art. The 'harvesters' vase and some frescoes in Mycenae also show people in that peculiar posture. As is well-known, Mycenae was deeply influenced by Crete. Yet Greek dancers of Mycenae do not carry themselves with a hollow back. In the present day only the flamenco dancers of Andalucia, together with Spanish bullfighters, have preserved this posture in dancing and in bullfighting. It is an essential pose in Spanish bullfighting, otherwise the man might get gored by the animal's horns!

Crete appears to be the only source from which this posture could have derived. It is possible that Cretan influence was taken along the shores of the northern Mediterranean and to Tartessos, and this tradition was kept up by the Gaditaneans. King Minos' fleets traded up and down the Inland Sea and took much more with them than visible goods! The Minoans founded colonies along the coasts of what is now southern France, Spain and Portugal. Bullfighting is still practised in those regions, but of course there are differences now.

In Portugal, although killing the bull is no longer allowed by law, bullfights still take place in summer. At times they have the Spanish way of a rider placing darts (banderillas) in the neck of the bull, but that is relatively rare. Usually nine men get in a long line, the leader attracting the bull by calling it and waving his arms about. When the bull charges the leader grips the animal's horns, somersaults over them onto the back of the astounded beast while the other eight men grab the ears, tail and forelegs of the bull and bring it to a sudden standstill. When the astonished bull raises his head, the leader gives a sharp order, all the men let go, the leader vaults off backwards and off goes the bull at a gallop. This piece of acrobatics is repeated several times, then the animal is let loose. This is called a *pega* (hold). In Spain a bullfight is different. As the bull charges into the ring, the *capeador* (man with a cape) plays it to see whether it is a right-handed or a left-handed animal. If left-handed it is dangerous, and the bull can toss the fighter if he is not on his guard. Five minutes later the *rejoneador* (lancer) comes on and gores the bull's neck near the shoulder blades to make it keep its head down. Five minutes later the *banderillo* drives three pairs of *banderillas* into the neck near the shoulder blades. This is to infuriate the bull. So far the bullfighters are on the ground except the *rejoneador* who rides a horse which is blindfolded on the side of the bull, and with a protective armour in case the bull should want to gore it. Then comes the *maestro* with a pointed sword, and after playing the bull he thrusts the sword between the shoulder blades to hit the heart. All this should be done in fifteen minutes, and what a gory performance it is. But the French of Provence love it, and although killing bulls is forbidden in France, Spanish fighters are invited in, the fine is paid and the killing goes on – because the public ask for it. . . On some feast days up to eight bulls are killed in one afternoon.

In the villages bullfighting is different. Bulls too tame or too old to fight are brought to a plaza, the young men play the bulls with their jackets or a scarf, and after about half an hour, the bulls are taken away, led by tame bullocks. These animals are taken to another village where more young men play them. These bulls are called *vaquillas* (heifers) but, of course, they are not heifers but bulls.

The protocol may change a little as one moves northwards in Spain, but the gripping atmosphere of the bull festivals is striking even today in such cities as Pamplona (Navarre), Bilbao and San Sebastian (the Basque country), Estella and Burgos, Logroño and Soria (Castile), where the town vibrates with a delirium not encountered in other festivals. Even hobby-bulls made up on wheelbarrows and masques thrill the crowds. A sort of enchanted cloak descends upon you during a bull festival. No doubt some of the Mithraic beliefs and rites propagated all over the Roman world by its legions have left something to posterity.

But we are a long way from flamenco.

When clapping is an element of the dance, both hands should be held curved and slightly to the left of the face (never in front of the face) while clapping at shoulder level. The face expresses the 'soul' of the dance, therefore it should be visible to everyone. If the dance is to express joy, as in the *Alegrías*, then the dancer should smile. If the dance is meant to show sadness and how the dance drives that sentiment away, the face should show that, too. The hands must have the middle and third fingers touching, curved inwards a little, the first finger and little finger should be separate from the middle two, and the thumb extended. The *right* hand should have the little finger and thumb separate from the three middle fingers. These three should be curved and touching each other. When a 'sharp' clap is required, the tips of the right hand touch the base of the first and middle fingers, making loud claps. The way to obtain muted claps (to keep time, for example, or to indicate the speed to the musician), is to slide the right hand forward so that both palms are opposite each other, all fingers curved, the fingers of the right hand overlapping between first finger and thumb of the left hand. One needs practice for this.

Where to look when dancing

An essential rule is to look at your partner, for the reason one dances with a partner is to get to know him/her. Dancing induces a form of euphoria which brings friendship and understanding between dancers. In all social dances this looking at one's partner is essential. Dancing is an opportunity to get to know new people. Don't look up at the ceiling, as so many badly taught ballet dancers do, for that breaks contact with your partner and your audience; and don't look at the floor either, except occasionally to accentuate a special step. Andalucian dances are usually complicated and require agility. Older people cannot always continue to participate, but they love to watch. Therefore a solo dancer should perform for his audience as well. Knowing that he is appreciated and admired helps the dancer to perform better. It gives him 'spirit', *el duende*, as the Andalucians say. This spiritual rapport between performer and spectator unites them so everyone benefits from the performance.

A solo dancer should express the spirit of the dance, and if it is an *Alegrías* (happy dance) joy shoud be expressed in the facial features. It is deadening to watch an *Alegrías* being performed by a serious dancer without a glimmer of joy in his or her face. Or if dancing a *Tientos* (sad solo dance to rid oneself of sorrowful thoughts) do not perform with a smile on your face, but show the suffering that you started with and gradually become happy. In reality, if you *feel* a dance you can express it properly.

A couple dance without a smile is a dead exercise, just as it is when dancers look at the floor all the time. The performance is no longer a dance but only a physical exercise to music. It gives no joy or special satisfaction. Social folk dances are meant to bring euphoria to all and make people forget their daily worries. Throw yourself into the dance!

Distance between partners

Partners should be just far enough apart to be able to join hands when standing opposite one another. But of course they don't join hands, convention does not allow this! But you must not stand too far from each other, for if you do there is no relationship between you; you might as well dance solos. The idea of dancing with a partner is to get to know each other, and to speak together in the dance if so wished.

Touching toes

In some dances partners, facing, have to extend one leg towards their partner and thus their toes should touch. It is a step created for this purpose: in order to get more familiar with one's partner. If toes are far apart, there is no point in the movement. Young people are frequently extremely shy, especially in the country, so certain movements were created to break down this shyness.

After dancing with a partner

When the dance is over, it is customary not to just abandon your partner and go your way, but for the man to offer his right hand to his partner, palm upwards, while she places her left hand, palm downwards, into his palm. The hands should be waist high, not in the air, or thigh level, as they are apt to be with some awkward people. Then the man conducts his partner back to a chair with a word of thanks. Up till the Civil War in Spain, girls had to be conducted back safely to their mothers or chaperones – that was 'proper'.

Holding the skirt

When you have to hold your skirt during a dance, girls, remember to take it up not from the front, nor from the side, but lean forward a little, bend and pick it up between front and side, knee level, and bring it up either to waist level at both sides, or with one hand at waist level, the other a little lower. Either way, both hands should have the back of the hand towards the body. Or if you are already dancing, extend both arms forward, curved, with the hands a little apart, the wrists forward, and all the fingers (except the forefinger and thumb which hold the skirt) spread out in a fan-shape. The wrists should move slightly and gently back and forth in time to the music, but the arms should be *slightly curved throughout the dance.* Hold yourself upright, with an arched back, shoulders down, the elbows away from the body. The arms must never be straight, but they must emulate the crescent moon, or horns of the sacred bull god for good luck (for the crops need rain and sun, and that is why those movements were created in dance form). In recent times girls have forgotten how to hold their skirts. They either hold them very high, to the side so one can see their petticoats all the time, or just in front, a little below the waist, with closed fists as if they were furious, or frightened, or with straight, meaningless arms, and these postures make them look awkward and bad dancers – which they are.

SOME CHARACTERISTICS OF THE DANCES IN VARIOUS PROVINCES

Dance styles are bound to differ from region to region. We can glance at some of the characteristics of the various districts in Spain, so we can know what to expect.

In mountainous regions the favourite steps are jumping, skipping, leaping, hopping, kicking ones, because the climate not only allows this form of exercise but seems to demand active moments. In hotter regions, walking steps and quieter interpretations of the same or similar themes are indulged in. The figures may be similar, the aims of the dance may also be similar, but the interpretation will certainly be different. Climate and geography influence style. Clothes will be lighter, or heavier, according to the climate of the district. There are also the various influences brought into a district by invading peoples who settled in a particular region, and these also influence style and costume. Small wonder then that there is so much variety. Throughout history these factors have played their part in forming the traditions of a region. In some peripheral districts, styles will combine in the one dance. For example, in the *Seguidillas Murcianas* (Murcia), the verses combine the southern smooth type of steps like an Andalucian dance, with the hopping steps and figures of Aragón, further north. On the other hand the *pas-de-Basque* is found all over the Peninsula – styles may differ, but it is still a *pas-de-Basque*.

The arms raised, held a little forward in a crescent-moon shape (or bull's horns), are found all over the Peninsula except in Andalucia and Cataluña. In Andalucia the Moors left their Persian style of movement of hips, shoulders, arms and hands (the latter in imitation of snakes). In Cataluña, the

Greeks left their imprint in the movements of the arms. Horizontal, curved, moving gradually from left to right and back again, the wrists flicking round in time to the beats of the music, while the fingers are fan-shaped, curved, the wrists pushed forward like birds. The way the girls hold their skirts in Cataluña is as follows: they pick up the skirt between finger and thumb, knee-level but neither well to the side nor in front of the knee. They raise the hands slightly forward and outward, and during the dance the flexible wrists move backwards and forwards in time to the music, the fingers always being in a fan-like shape. This style appears to have come from medieval times when the Courts of Love in southern France spread to European courts, and Cataluña at the time belonged to southern France (as it is now called!). Unfortunately, I have noticed that Catalan girls now hold their skirts very badly as a rule. They are not taught as we were in 1926–36, when correct positioning of the various parts of the body was an essential part of folk dance in Cataluña. Everybody had to dance on their toes, and the steps were neatly performed both by men and women. The only dance in Cataluña which contained arm positions in a crescent-moon shape was the Sardana in which anyone who wished took part, men and women alternately, in concentric circles either in a public square or in the streets or on the threshing floors. Otherwise the arms were held shoulder-high only, or down to the sides (for the men). This posture of the arms and hands in Cataluña is believed to derive from Greek influence, for the Greeks founded several colonies along the coast and left many of their beliefs, such as the wrist movements connected with the dove, the bird of Aphrodite, goddess of love.

There are ritual dances for men and others for women, and in Castelltersol (north of Barcelona) there are two for both men and women. At midsummer the *Bal del Ciri* (candle dance) is performed in church, with the six couples concerned carrying a lit candle and a glass jar filled with perfume and adorned with ribbons. At the end of the dance all go to the porch and the men throw the jars onto neighbouring roofs, where they break and the perfume trickles down onto the crowds below. This is rain magic, or asking for rain for the crops. The second dance is in front of the church and there sun worship figures are performed. Thus, both rain and sun are invoked for good harvests.

Maypole dances – like our English ones – are alive along the coast, and both the men and the girls recite verses during the dance with implications of courtship. We know that the sacred Tree is revered in most parts of the world as a life-giving and a fertility-granting deity. Other districts of Spain also have maypole dances, all with ribbons that are entwined down the mast, and in Portugal there is one version where a kind of hut is woven, with a roof as distinct from the 'walls', all made of ribbons – very clever! In some dances the girls carry a fan and promenade while their partners process out of the dance space, fetch a bunch of flowers each, and present them to their partner before dancing off. In another dance they give the girls special bread shaped like rings and place these over the girls' arms during the dance, then they all go off to enjoy the food! There are the usual 'bridge' figures, encountered in every country, as well as weavers' dances evolved in most European countries.

In most of Spain and Portugal dances take place in the village streets, because there is no hall large enough to hold everybody – so the dances take the form of two long rows. A few dances require sixteen dancers, for they were based on four, multiplied by four – both sacred numbers. I have not found anywhere more than one dance for a solo, or for one couple, in Cataluña. Those were the *Hereu Riera* for one man hopping over crossed sticks – just like the Scottish Argyll Broadswords and English Bacca-pipe Jig. And the other was the *Morisca* for a couple, the man pursuing his partner, said to be Moorish.

The only dance known to all Catalans is the *Sardana* which

is performed in rings of alternate men and women with linked little fingers. They dance in the main square or in the streets, and go on for hours on end. It is a grave dance, moving to left then to right, accompanied by a *cobla* (band) of ten wind instruments and one double bass. Up to the middle of the last century only one shawm, a flute and a drum were used. Each village has its own *esbart* (dance club), and the Sardana has local variants, but competitions are organised for Sardanas once a year in Barcelona.

Galicia, the north-western province of Spain, has a favourite dance called the *Muinheira* (the miller's wife). Anything that has to do with a miller, his wife or his daughter, or the baker, is sacred, because of their connection with grain and therefore fertility. There are dances called *La Boulangère* in France, or *La Bolangera* in Cataluña, and there may be similar dances in other countries. *Le Meunier* and *La Meunière* in France indicate how important those people were who were connected with *food*, a subject of paramount importance. There are many places in Spain where dances, or ritual acts, are performed on the threshing floors. One such example is in San Pedro Manrique, where at midsummer the Mayor and Corporation beat the bounds, after the fire festival of the previous evening, and salute the three *Móndidas* (priestesses) who carry a basket with loaves on their heads. The threshing floor is the last place where the salutation takes place.

The bagpipe and drum are the traditional instruments in Galicia for dance accompaniments. Occasionally, for a ritual dance, a marine conch is also used.

Galicia, like most provinces, has many longways and circular dances, but both sexes perform the same steps – except, of course, for the ritual dances. The steps are lively with hops and jumps. Men's ritual dances exist but they are not as numerous as further east, in Cantabria.

Since Galicia has a long coastline, fishermen's dances naturally are performed. The figures are the usual ones found

Móndida

The Móndida of Anguiano is one of the three priestesses that bring fertility to the crops. The branches in her basket are covered in yellow dough – colour of the sun. Three loaves of bread support them. The roses round her basket signify womanhood and are always red (the colour of life). Her white skirt is lace. Her blouse is also white, but the shawl is red. She carries a fan in her hand – for conveying messages, as she is unable to move her head much with the basket on it.

in our Morris dances, but in a couple of villages such as Redondella they carry long cords, the ends of which are held by the captain, in the lead. All face the same way, and the dancers hold on to the cords which are over the shoulders of the captain. After some steps in place, they cast off (the ram's horns figure) and dance back to place in their four long rows. Sixteen men take part in this one. Further south there are two other fishermen's dances, with complicated figures, including a spiral in single file (the spiral means 'creation'). But I have not seen them.

Asturias, east of Galicia, has much in common with it. For instance the bagpipe and drum are the chief instruments, even in the depths of the country. Hops, jumps and side kicks are numerous and complicated. The arms are held up in the crescent-moon style, and they use half-moon figures, ellipses, V-shapes, and the circle. There is also a solemn dance called the *Danza Prima* (chief dance), where everyone joins hands in a single sideways file, and dances along the streets, winding along in a continuous snaky pattern. The steps are simple: one step forward onto the right foot, step back onto the left. Step back onto the right foot, a little to the side, then step back onto the left foot, towards the right foot. And so on, round the town. The arms are jerked forwards and backwards together with the feet, the leader sings the verses and the chorus joins in. Professor Eduardo Torner explains that this dance was originally round a shrine, a sacred stone or pillar, or round a tree, or idol. It sounds as if he were right – except for the song, which has nothing sacred about it as it tells the sad story of a forlorn love-sick maiden. (Although the chorus goes 'Long live our Lady Virgin of Carmen'. . .) Torner describes the song and gives the music in an article in *Folklore de España* (vol. II, Carreras y Candi).

Asturias has another fertility dance. When a field is ploughed and ready to be sown, a row of women – usually nine – comes onto the field holding evergreen twigs in their hands, and they shuffle along across the field, while a solitary man dancer (representing the Wise Man) performs leaps, high jumps, twists and turns in the air with intricate steps, in front of the women. He is said to show the crops how high they must grow. This is the *Pericote* (Little Peter). Another version is performed by one man and two women. These last face, shuffle towards each other, move past the partner, and make a bow, back to back, retreating to place, thus making a figure of eight as a ground pattern, while the man crosses over their figure, as soon as they are back in place. He stamps, twists and makes intricate steps. Of course, there are men's ritual dances here, too, and they carry sticks and wear flowers on their hats, as is customary all over Europe for ritual dancers.

Cantabria, west of the Basque country, is a mountainous region and it possesses a wealth of ancient dances, both ritual and social. The men's ritual dances are similar to our Morris dances, even to the costume in white with baldrick and bell-pads. Steps and figures are also the same. The difference comes in when men carry two sticks instead of one only, as in English Morris. Some Cantabrian sword dances have wooden swords instead of metal ones. In many of the ritual dances it is the girls who provide the accompaniment, strumming on their tambourines and singing, instead of the usual shawm and drum. The tambourine is a woman's instrument as it represents the moon. Cantabrian ritual dancers are called *Picayos*, and they often dance in churches.

The Basques, on both sides of the Pyrenees, have a great variety of steps. Some require great agility, the kicks being higher than any other dance requirements in any country! Some dances have shields and swords. These are, of course, the Christians and Moors, or derivations of these.

There are also mummers' plays, and death and resurrection dances, such as in Berriz where the leader suddenly throws himself backwards horizontally, is caught by two dancers, and is held stiff and horizontal during a dance by his followers. Then he suddenly comes to life again. Or at Lequeitio, where a man dances on a coffin carried by two men, shoulder high. On the French side a wonderful hobby-horse dance takes place, where the 'horse' is castrated, 'dies', then comes back to life, ending with tremendous leaps and jumps, even over the other dancers who kneel down for the purpose. This wonderful *Mascarade* takes place in La Soule valley. The principal characters have to stand on one foot on a glass half filled with wine, and they must not upset the glass nor spill a drop! The horse wears glittering jacket and gaiters, like his four followers, so no wonder they are called *Les Beaux* (the beautiful ones). Their red and white costume is embroidered with gold thread and sequins. They look wonderful, and the horse-dancer wears a huge head-dress covered in flowers. Their counterparts *Les Noirs* (the black ones) are dirty and sooty and show that the Mascarade is evidently a death and resurrection dance representing the renewal of spring after the death of winter. The whole performance was meant to remind the deities not to forget to revive nature.

Another version of a ritual death theme takes place in *Navarre*. After a sword dance by eight or six men, the captain either has all the sticks – or swords – stuck round his neck, or he climbs onto a platform of swords or sticks and is hoisted up shoulder-level, then suddenly brought down again – but without harm nowadays! Unlike what happens in Ibio, where the captain (or really the surrogate captain) has the leader's sword pointed against his body and suddenly all the lances which were supporting him are withdrawn with a jerk, and he falls to the ground – unharmed nowadays, but in olden times he was killed. This dance in Ibio is made all the more eerie by the marine conch wailing its doleful notes to the accompaniment of the drum. It is a frightening dance, in spite of the spectators knowing that no harm will come to the dancer in question. In Navarre, south of the Basque country, numerous ritual men's dances exist, very similar to the

Basque ones, with lots of jumps, leaps and high kicks. The girls have less spectacular steps and figures than the men, and they must look down on the ground and be shy! Also they expect the men to dance before them and kneel down to ask them to come and be their partner – like the Cantabrians and the Basques.

In *the Pyrenees* near the French frontier, for example at Ochagavía, the dancers perform for *Nuestra Señora de Muskilda* (Our Lady of the Dew, or of Sowing the Seed). In the evening they dance in the main square, and next morning early they climb to the Lady's shrine on top of the sacred hill. After Mass, the dancers display their dances which contain figures very similar to our Morris dances. This is done before the Statue of Our Lady. The Fool, wearing his double mask depicting an old man in front and a young one at the back, dances best of all! He wears the Janus and Vesta mask of the Old and New Years – frequent in the Peninsula. The dancers wear white knee breeches, an embroidered skull cap, a white shirt and a vast quantity of coloured embroidered ribbons hanging from the neck to the waist. Each man carries two sticks. After several dances, they go some fifty yards down the hill to an ancient, sacred oak tree, which is encased in a cement covering to protect it. It is said to be a thousand years old. It is obvious that the festival was originally for the worship of the tree or of the Earth Mother, in the sacred grove, so prevalent in archaic times. The whole hillside was covered in oak trees, but recently the little town sold the oaks to pay for a new water system, so the authorities had the region replanted with pines, for they grow quicker than oaks! The ancient ancestor was the only one saved. At Leiza the white-clad Morris men dance on a low wall, built on either side of the river that runs through the centre of the town. It seemed very dangerous to me as they leapt and turned on the narrow walls, but my fears were groundless. They danced beautifully. The instruments among the Basques and Navarrese are a drum and flute called Txistu and Tabalet.

Social dances are similar to those in Quipuzcoa – that is, the men leap about and kick high, and are most ceremonious towards their partner – not surprising, for all the northern regions remained under the matriarchal system for several hundred years after the southern parts had adopted patriarchy and the worship of the sun (as opposed to matriarchy, which followed the moon worship of their ancestors). *Jotas* are also danced in the north but are said to have come from Aragón. *Fandangos* are also a favourite, but are supposed to have originated in Andalucia, where, as soon as someone sings, the others dance, or vice versa, so a fandango can be a song or a dance, or both. Both jotas and fandangos are couple dances.

One of the ritual dances of the Navarrese is the *Sagar Dantza* (Apple Dance). Four men, wearing white trousers and shirts and very tall pointed hats covered with paper flowers, carry an apple in each hand. They dance in the streets 'to bring good luck' to the community. The apple is the fruit of the north, just as cider is the drink of the north. It was the sacred fruit.

Some fifty years ago a priest called Padre Donostia felt sorry for the girls, who had few dances of their own, so he invented an apple dance for them. They carry baskets of apples on their heads – surely not good to dance with! – and cross over to opposite sides with their girl partner with a walking step. They can't do anything else because of the weight. How foolish to invent such a meaningless dance!

Aragonese dances are performed with intricate skips, jumps and crisscrossing of the legs. All the steps are either hops or skips, for social and ritual dances. The climate demands movement, for it can be very cold in the mountains of Aragón. The ritual dances for men are reminiscent of Morris dances, with sometimes six, but usually eight, men in sets of four. One dance figures boys on the men's shoulders, making a kind of tower. Presumably they represent higher spirits, or a powerful deity. Such towers are found in Turkey and Morocco as well as in Tarragona and in Vallés (western

Cataluña), but there with up to nine storeys. Sitges (Cataluña) has also kept up this tradition, only there they make Biblical tableaux, keeping up pagan traditions mixed in with the Biblical ones. It is generally supposed that jotas are strictly Aragonese. This is not so. Jotas are performed in most of the Peninsula, and Castile is rife with jotas. They are always in 3/4 or 3/8 time.

The Central Plateau. This region is most colourful in costumes, which are extremely rich in embroideries, as well as in the way jewellery is made and worn. We shall describe some later. The dances contain hopping and jumping steps as well as walking ones, but the figures are intricate at times. The arms are held high in a crescent-moon shape, and the dancers place themselves either in two rows, facing, or in circles, or in individual couples. There are the men's ritual dances, which are extremely interesting and complicated. Of course, their figures are similar to our Morris dances since the aims are the same, but there are more steps, and the men often wear petticoats with lace, starched knickers and colourful sashes; some wear crowns, and altogether they are fascinating. Ribbons are frequent as well, for through them the dancers are united with the various parts of the universe according to the colour; for example, red for love and life, green for regeneration of nature, blue for sky and purity, yellow and orange for the sun and wisdom, white for innocence and purity. It appears that the colours have the same significance everywhere.

Aragón has had some influence in rhythm and leaps and hops, and the jota is a dance found everywhere, though each one is different from the others.

Let us now go south to the Mediterranean coast, to *Valencia*, that very rich province of the great river Ebro. Here, an amalgamation of styles incorporates Catalan grace, some Aragonese steps and a few hops, and some Andalucian steps, which have evolved into charming dances.

Ritual dances exist as usual, with similar figures to the

Morris dances, but a particular flavour of their own. Some are extremely intricate and spectacular in rhythm like the costumes. Valencia being the first district along the coast to receive the blessings of silk production from the Near East, the costumes are made of silk damask – satin for the men – with gold embroidery and gold sequins mixed with pearls galore. These last are sewn onto the white lace aprons and shawls. The women wear tall combs of copper, silver or gold, and side combs, too, with silver pins to hold the plaited chignon at the back, wonderful gold earrings and a brooch embossed with precious stones on the breast. Pearl fishing was an ancient practice among the Persian Gulf fishermen and also the Greeks, who taught the natives of Valencia how to do it, and this custom still prevails in the Bay of Valencia. Pearls mean 'new life', which was why Aphrodite came out of a shell: she was the new life, the pearl, coming into being.

Valencia, with its abundance of fruit, rice fields and regular irrigation (organised by the Moors), is a rich province indeed. In the hills, the peasants wear richly embroidered dark waistcoats and breeches and a cocked hat. All the men carry a wonderful striped blanket over the shoulder in lieu of an overcoat – which is not usually the custom among the peasantry. On feast days the costumes are just glorious for men as well as for women.

To accompany their dances, pipe (*dulzaina*) and drum are the usual instruments, although the guitar gets mixed up with some bands – this influence coming from Andalucia.

If we go over to the *Balearic Islands* we find Catalan grace and language, but the steps and figures are all their own. These islands have received influences from the numerous cultures that invaded them, and they have made this mixture into a charming combination. In a dance for two women and one man (we have come across some similar examples before), the *Parado de Valdemosa*, the dancers bend down and draw a circle round themselves with the forefinger 'to prevent evil from coming near them'. A favourite dance there is the Well Dance when young people meet at the fountain or well after work. Or they meet under the eaves of an arbour covered with vines that provide shade from the fierce sun. Ritual dances are the Eagle Dance, as in other parts of Spain, though each version differs from all the others, of course. The instruments used are the guitar, the flute or shawm, drum and castanets.

Andalucia. Why is this province called so? This dates from the time of the Visigothic invasions from the north in the fifth and sixth centuries AD. The Vandals came down and settled in the south, so it became the 'Land of the Vandals': Vandalucia, or Andalucia now.

The guitar was introduced into Andalucia by the Moors, and this instrument quickly spread from there to most of Europe. Andalucia was greatly influenced by Moorish arts, song style and dance, but the underlying culture still remains in outlying districts.

In the southern district of Andalucia, the arms are mostly raised above the head (both curved all the time to emulate the horns of the bull-god), but one arm comes out, down, round and up again across the body, to join the other arm, which remains above the head and slightly back, to accentuate the hollow back which is essential in Andalucian dance style. Then the other arm goes round making a circle in its turn, to join the arm above the head. If castanets are used, then the palms of the hands must be kept facing the ground (except when they clash together), so that the two lobes of the castanets are kept apart – otherwise they will not strike properly. But if no castanets are used, then the hands and fingers must be curved, separated, and move round the wrist. That is, the wrist should be twisted round in a continuous movement to emulate the movement and twists of a snake, for that was the origin of the hand movements in flamenco dancing. This custom came from Persia, via the Moors. When the Arabs conquered Persia the women learnt those movements from Persian women, for they – and the ancient Greeks – worshipped snakes, as they still do in India and parts of Asia. This custom followed when the use of live snakes was discontinued and hand and arms took the place of these sacred beasts. As the Moorish traditions and style became amalgamated with the local style of southern Andalucia, so the tradition now called *Flamenco* was evolved. In no part of the rest of the Iberian Peninsula is this tradition the accepted norm. One only sees flamenco dancing in the rest of Spain in taverns in cities and towns, or in nightclubs, for tourists.

In Delphi, in classical Greek times, the oracle was a python and the virgin who looked after this snake was called the Pythoness. When the worship of live snakes fell into disuse, she became the oracle. In parts of Greece women used to worship live snakes which they kept in holes in the ground, but this custom died out in time. In Morocco and among North American Indians, however, snake worship is still extant. Some African tribes still worship snakes. The women hold each other by the hips, in a long line, and move in a wavy-line along the dance space, emulating the movements of a snake. There may also be other forms of snake dances.

The style of Andalucian song called *Jondo* is also said to have come from Persia, where this type of voice production, as well as the arm movements, are still to be seen.

Further inland from the Mediterranean coast, in the hills, the dances are not of flamenco style but seem to contain much older traditions, more like the dances found further north, with hops and jumps. Flamenco is not practised here.

Seguidillas are 'little verses that follow one another'. They are couple dances. The southern half of the Peninsula has seguidillas both for song and dance, though each district, or village, has its own version. The best known ones are the *Seguidillas Sevillanas*, presumably because Seville has a pilgrimage renowned all over the Peninsula. Each seguidilla has its own type of steps and figures quite different from one another. The dances usually consist of three parts to each of the four verses. In the north there are dances containing three verses also, but they are called *Figuras*, not seguidillas. In Andalucia, where they speak extremely fast and consequently leave out consonants, they just say *Seguiryas*, and call it a different type of dance. Stage arrangements have converted this couple dance into solos for women – which is a great pity.

The guitar accompanied the songs and dances evolved in that part of the country. The snake-like arm and hand movements imitating the twists of snakes by the women who worshipped these reptiles in the Near, Middle and Far East, were kept up by the women in their dances, long after their origins had been forgotten. Andalucia is the only province of Spain that preserves these movements. The arms are always curved, and moved in a circle, usually one after the other. The right arm performs the active, masculine circle: out, down, across the body, up above the head and slightly back, while the left arm remains up waiting for the right arm to join it. Then the left arm performs a similar circle: the passive, feminine side. Thus both arms complement each other and a 'perfect whole' is achieved. The fingers meanwhile move round one after the other, down, up and out, like a wheel, the wrists following. A beautiful movement. The back must be slightly hollow, the chest out, shoulders down and chin in. The shoulders shake from side to side quickly at times, the hips move sideways, so the dance movements are enticing.

The style of singing taken over by the Arabs from the Persians, and the voluptuous body movements of the East, were retained also. But what was not inherited from the East was the footwork. The *zapateado* (shoe-work) derived from stamping to waken the spirits of the underworld, as we have seen earlier, was brought over by Neolithic peoples from the Near East, with their agriculture and rituals.

Flamenco – as that type of dance is now called – is a most exciting style of dance, but it requires a smooth wooden floor or a hard stone surface to be shown to its best advantage.

Unfortunately, the dance as displayed in taverns and nightclubs nowadays is so mutilated by stage arrangements that the full range of the original flamenco style has been lost. This is a tragedy; the immense variety and colour performed up to the Civil War in Spain, has been muted and modified until it has lost much of its meaning. Do any of the old dancers still remember the old style and the dances? Will they be able to revive old dances?

The province of *Extremadura*, north of Andalucia and west to the Portuguese frontier, has been influenced greatly by Andalucia. but owing to mountainous and therefore cold terrain, the costumes are mostly very thick, and the dances contain hops and jumps, leaps and intricate steps. Some dances are very interesting. As usual they are divided between the ritual and the social, including courting dances. Up the mountains and away from large towns, the people have kept up the ancient dance styles from archaic times, tempted only by some Andalucian influence (which contains Moorish traces anyway). The ritual dances, although diverse in general, always contain the same aims – requests for rain, for sun, for good luck, for good harvests and good catches of fish, or for new life.

THE ORIGINS OF FLAMENCO

Before 4000 to 3000 BC traders along the Mediterranean coasts travelled far and wide. They came for skins and amber. They brought eastern textiles and fruits. When metals were discovered and worked, these were bartered for north European goods – skins and amber – and later for metal ore such as tin, silver, copper and gold.

Colonies were founded along the coast, traces of which we can still see and admire. In the extreme south-west of the Peninsula a huge mine was found at what is now called

Huelva. A most important colony flourished, in those days named Tarshish or Tartessos; the open-cast mines are worked to this day. Traders came from Egypt, Palestine, Syria, Phoenicia, Greece; later from Marseilles, and still later from Carthage. They all came for metal ore, in exchange for eastern silks, jewellery, metal knives and swords, etc. Pliny the Elder tells us that at a time of famine in Rome, all the foreigners were expelled except the two thousand artists – musicians and dancers – from Tartessos. This means that they were so much appreciated by the Roman aristocracy that they could not do without those artists! Why were they so much loved? Presumably because their styles of dancing and playing instruments, and singing, were better than those of other nations. This was understandable since, because of the numerous different races that congregated in and around Tartessos, the traditions of many nations had amalgamated into something exceptionally sophisticated and beautiful, not found in other regions. The art of Tartessos was much admired before the advent of Christ.

In or about 1447 AD an influx of gypsies came to the Peninsula. Some had settled in Egypt before that – hence their name in Spanish – *Gitanos* (Egyptians); in French *Gitanes*, and in English *Gypsy*.

The question is, where did the gypsies originally come from? Their language is of Indian origin. Some authorities tell us that in India along the Indus Valley, at Harrapa and at Mojendro Daro, ruins of large brick buildings were found, with skeletons of dead warriors helter skelter, who had never received proper burial. It was surmised that these cities had been subjected to invaders who had killed many of the inhabitants and put the rest to flight. It is believed that these and other such refugees fled westwards, since Egypt had received gypsies late in its history. Europe received them later still. Gypsies are 'travellers' still, all over Europe. They are nomads who go the rounds of a particular region every year, staying some months before moving on to another favourite district. Thus they keep their animals fed, and are able to keep themselves alive without coming into disfavour by remaining too long in one district. These gypsies have kept up part of their language and some of their customs, which can be recognised wherever they go.

These tribes or families have acquired some of the languages of their hosts, as well as some of their customs. For instance, in France they have learnt French, in Germany German, and so on. They have learnt the tastes of their hosts, and have tried to manufacture things most likely to sell, such as baskets, posies, and such like. The women tell fortunes, the men are often tinkers or tin-smiths, and do repair work. They also breed horses and sell them. In some places gypsies dance at fairs, or sell trinkets. In Andalucia (southern Spain) they learnt that people danced in taverns or in the open, and sang and played the guitar, so little by little they also learnt to dance, sing and play the guitar as the Andalucians do. When I lived in Spain from 1926 to 1936, very few gypsies danced or sang in taverns; they had not learnt how from the Spaniards.

How was it that flamenco was practised all over Andalucia? Because the Moors had brought the style from Persia – where they had learnt that kind of dance – bringing it into an artistic and well-developed region that had already evolved its own dances, thanks to the numerous traders and visitors who had come to its coasts in the past. One can still see the snake-like movements of arms, hands and fingers in northeastern Persia today, as well as hear the cante jondo style of singing, and of course the guitar which the Moors had brought into Europe via Spain, when they came in 711 AD – long before the gypsies ever thought of coming to Andalucia.

Naturally it took time for the gypsies to learn to dance and sing in the proper flamenco style, for the simple reason that, being poor, they could not afford proper lessons, and so had to learn from watching where they could. Only very few gypsies can perform this art form. Were it part of their inheritance and custom, *something* of the style of dance and song would be apparent in all gypsy tribes wherever they lived, be it Scotland, France, Scandinavia, Ireland, England or Italy; but now, even in the rest of the Spain (outside Andalucia) gypsies do not know anything about flamenco. While I lived in Spain, except in a couple of taverns in Barcelona and Seville, gypsies were not familiar with flamenco. They just tried to imitate, and that very badly. A friend and I wanted to learn flamenco dancing from a gypsy, and went to a famous one called 'La Faraona'. It was hopeless; La Faraona knew so little, we had to find Spaniards in order to learn.

Walter Starkie, of the British Council in Madrid, went to the Balkans to learn flamenco from the gypsies there only to find they had acquired the art from Hungarian, Bulgarian or Yugoslav gypsies, who knew nothing whatever about flamenco dancing or singing. Had it been part of their inheritance, they would have known *something*. They did not, then. They had acquired fine Hungarian or Bulgarian styles of musicianship and dance.

Inland from the coast, in the hills of Andalucia, remote villages still keep up their ritual dances, in a similar fashion to the Morris dances. The social dances do not comprise flamenco, but they are charming in their own way. 'Walking' steps are the norm, not hopping steps – the warm climate precludes the latter.

The flamenco-style dances are hard to learn and take a long time to master properly. They are usually solos or couple dances, and are performed mostly in towns, not so much in the country districts. The country dance type, such as the *Seguidillas Sevillanas*, the *Seguidillas Malagueñas* and other seguidillas and fandangos from other towns, are all different, with enchanting figures, possessing their own individual styles. The rhythms are usually to be counted as in six movements (or beats) to make 'one' step – according to Andalucian dancers – although the musical timing is in ¾ or at times 3/8. This characteristic is also sometimes met in dances from the Near East.

Many dances are accompanied by song as well as the guitar in most parts of the Peninsula. Most social or courting dances comprise couples making symbolic figures such as the half moon; the sinuous snaky line, the zig-zag (water symbol); the circle (unity of the community); the ellipse (symbol of creation); some contain the figure of eight (eternity) and the square. Some dances are formed in two long rows of facing partners, or partners in sets of two or three couples, as well as individual couples not in sets or rows.

The most recent form of flamenco dancing is found in the so-called flamenco dancing for the stage. This type has been choreographed by dancing masters who draw their inspiration from folk dances. The stage knows nothing of the original meanings of figures, so they mix up the figures regardless, so long as it is spectacular!

Nowadays it has become the fashion (thanks to tourists who look for the exotic) to wish to see flamenco dancing and singing performed by gypsies, since this would seem to them to be something out-of-the-way. So many Spaniards pretend to look like 'gypsies', and quite a few gypsies have now learnt flamenco, some having become good dancers, guitarists and singers; some are even good bullfighters! The best performers are, of course, the Spaniards, for it has been their tradition in Andalucia for some hundreds of years. The Spaniards it was who evolved the complicated footwork, zapateado, not the gypsies. So we find that the gypsies have earned a reputation they do not really deserve.

The fault lies chiefly with the Spanish people themselves. Before the Civil War, anything done in taverns was disreputable, and therefore someone who danced or performed in a tavern was *un gitano* – a gypsy, a no-good. What a pity, now that flamenco art is much prized, that the authorship should be attributed to people who neither invented nor evolved it!

PORTUGAL

In this country, dances are as charming as in Spain. This is not surprising since it is only since the twelfth and thirteenth centuries that Portugal has existed as a separate country. In the time of the Crusades, Prince Affonso Enriques, son of a Galician nobleman, crowned himself king of Portucalis (Oporto nowadays) while his father was fighting in the Near East. Affonso Enriques did not like the goings-on between his mother and a nobleman so he put her in a convent and went conquering the neighbourhood. His successors enlarged their territory southwards, in the course of time. But Portugal was re-conquered by a Spanish king, Philip II, so it received further influence from Spain during that time. Sixty years after, Portugal once more became independent.

Ritual dances for men exist here, too, side by side with social dances. A most fascinating ritual dance exists in Miranda do Douro, in the high mountains of the north-west. The performers wear embroidered, stiffly starched white skirts, a fancy embroidered waistcoat, a white shirt, a bright coloured 'Spanish' shawl embroidered with flowers round the waist, a flowered black hat with broad brim, ribbons down the back, striped stockings and black boots. They are expert dancers and carry two sticks each. Their figures are similar to those of our Morris dances. The river Douro starts in Spain and flows roughly from east to west, then it flows through Portugal into the sea at Oporto. All along its banks charming dances are performed, and the custom prevails in Portugal, without regard to frontiers. The costumes also are similar on both sides of the frontier, with their rich embroideries and colourful woven materials. In the northern province of Minho, the women's costumes are extraordinarily beautiful and colourful. The skirts are woven at home, with complicated vertical designs of different colours in between stripes. A white blouse with blue embroidery is worn under a bright red and black waistcoat, also lavishly embroidered with symbolic designs. Each village has its special fashion. Some skirts are edged with black, others with a red band, also embroidered, but most designs are symbolic. A bright red, orange or yellow shawl with fringes and printed flowers adorns the head, the two ends crossing at the nape of the neck, up the sides of the face, and tying on top of the head, the fringes framing the face. But the further south you go the simpler the costumes and the dances. The one exception for men is in the Ribatejo, north of Lisbon, where the cowboys are colourful in dark breeches, white stockings, a red waistcoat or a green one, and a red headbag. Very impressive.

Some dances are extremely simple, but all are very pleasant to dance. The instruments are mainly guitars, triangles, tambourines and, very occasionally, a flute. In the north-west, panpipes are still used, but nowadays only by knife grinders.

THE COCK

In Portugal the cock represents virility – as it does in the Near East – so it is the emblem of Portugal. For the New Year, children are given a clay cock, similar to this one – or a simplified version of this – and also of a goat, and they 'whistle in the New Year' to bring luck to all and to crops and herds.

CHAPTER FIVE

Costume in Spain, Portugal and Western Galicia

WE MUST JUST MENTION the costumes very briefly, for as each region has its own variants, it would need a whole book to give details of them all. We shall only mention a few of the most outstanding ones.

SPAIN

The richest and most ornate costumes are to be found in Castile and León, Salamanca outshining all the other provinces. The skirt is shaped like a half-moon, open at the back, but two wide, heavily embroidered bands hang from the waist to hide the join. The red or black woollen skirt is so heavily embroidered in coloured, gold and silver thread, that the cloth can hardly be seen. Appliqué designs are also used. The cloth apron often has a satin frill, but the rest is covered in embroidery, like the dark velvet bodice with long sleeves. Over the shoulders a velvet capelet is worn, also covered in jet, sequins and coloured embroidery, and over that a white lace shawl shows up the rich costume. This lace shawl is also covered in sequins. A white lace veil covers the head and ornate hair style. Two discs of hair cover the ears, and they are kept in place by twelve silver filigree pins. The whole front of the girl is covered with eight or ten huge necklaces of silver or gold globules or filigree beads. Amulets and crosses add to the richness of the costume. The wealth is unbelievable! White stockings of knitted lace and black shoes show off the whole outfit.

Alberca comes next in richness, together with the province of León – where several ornate petticoats of many colours are worn, together with innumerable necklaces coming down to the knees of the wearer.

The ladies of Armuña are also elaborate, but they wear straw hats covered in artificial flowers and many good luck symbols. Further south the women wear many brightly coloured cloth skirts, so when they dance they look like birds of paradise. The girls in Asturias and Galicia wear red cloth skirts, black velvet bodices and capelets, all lavishly covered in jet and black sequins, while those of Valencia prefer silk damask in pale colours, with quantities of flowered designs, white lace aprons and shawls all adorned with pearls, and gold thread in symbolic designs. Their copper, silver or gold combs are unique, as they tower above the head of the wearer. They look exquisitely refined and elegant. The simplest costumes are found in the Basque country, where plain red woollen skirts with a black band, a white blouse and red flannel bodice show off the fresh complexion of the wearers. A white kerchief covers the head and is knotted in the nape of the neck.

The Catalan girls wear plain damask skirts in pale colours, black satin bodices, mostly black lace aprons and lace fichus, and their characteristics are black lace mittens and a black lace headbag (as worn in the time of Goya), which men also wear at times under their flannel headbag – inherited from the Greek head-dress.

The Andalucian cities have the tradition of a pale silk dress – the skirt being a whole circle – with flounces on it. Some have only one flounce while others may have up to ten or twelve, each edged with a contrasting colour, or a lace frill. A silk shawl is worn over the shoulders and pinned on the breast with a rose (representing woman) or a carnation (representing man) to give an elegant finish to the dress. On great occasions they wear a large tortoiseshell comb, often with a black lace mantilla (in the case of a married woman) or a white lace one, in the case of an unmarried girl. This costume is most becoming. Unfortunately, a new fashion has recently cropped up among the gypsies – who cannot usually afford such elegant dresses – of wearing any flowered cotton skirt, a different type of bodice, and the shawl round the hips! A ridiculous custom, for the hips are never cold in warm weather, and a shawl is definitely not needed there. . . The sad part of this is that since those gypsies were seen in taverns, some people thought that it was the new fashion so they imitated this ugly style. Thus are traditions erased from memory and new meaningless items introduced into daily life. The flounced skirts of the 'Sevillanas' were so graceful, making the girls look like flowers.

When going out in the evenings, the women wore the so-called 'Spanish shawls', huge square silk wonders heavily embroidered with flowers and with very long fringes. These enormous shawls are made in Manila or China, not in Spain, so they are called *Manton de Manila* by the Spanish women. Beautiful they are, too.

PORTUGAL AND WESTERN GALICIA

These two regions are taken together because they speak practically the same language and Portugal as a political entity was only created in the twelfth century. Its ethnic background, character and social customs and fashions had already been formed long before that date. The northern part of Portugal belonged to the kingdom of León, whereas part of the south was under Moorish domination for some five hundred years before Portugal's independence.

It could be said that regional costumes of Portugal are, on the whole, not so rich in colour or in material as those of Spain. Notable exceptions are those of Braga, in the north, and those of Malpíca, in the east, along the Tagus valley down to Vilafranca de Xira (north of Lisbon). The costumes of Viana do Castelo, in the Minho region, are outstandingly rich. The skirts are handwoven in stripes of white, red, yellow, black, blue or green, according to the village, for each has its own particular order and width of stripe. The hem is a broad band of red or black flannel, usually embroidered with coloured wools and sequins – though a couple of villages have a plain black band. The main theme of the embroideries on the band is always a wavy line (meaning the water symbol) with flowers issuing out of the main stem. The bodices are sleeveless, usually of red flannel above and black velvet on the lower half of the bodice, but always heavily embroidered with symbolic designs and some sequins. The linen chemise is always adorned with blue flowers at the neck and on the shoulders, and the 'tapestry' apron is equally colourful; as usual, each village has its own particular designs, either flowered or with squares. This apron is not only woven in colours, but also embroidered in wools on top of the weaving. The whole effect is most striking. Viana do Castelo has been an important port for many centuries, and perhaps this brought prosperity to the surrounding countryside, hence the elaborate costumes. What is also interesting is that over the border in Galicia, a very similar costume is worn by the Spanish peasant women, because at one time both regions were united in one kingdom, although the usual costume for women in Galicia is a red skirt with black velvet bands near the hem. This is for unmarried girls; blue, green or yellow skirts for married women is the norm.

Another city where rich costumes are to be seen is Braga, in the north – once a royal residence and an important mountain fortress. Black cloth and velvet, heavily embroidered with jet and sequins, fill the onlooker with admiration. It is unusual for unmarried girl to wear black, which is usually reserved for brides and married women. Black is the colour of respectability, and a married woman must not attract attention to herself. An unmarried girl should catch the eye, for an unmarried girl is believed to represent a flower! Once she is married a woman must show her respectability by wearing dark colours only, or neighbours will want to know why! Exceptionally, unmarried girls in Braga wear black.

On the other hand, the peasantry of Malpíca is much influenced by Spanish customs because it is a border district with Spain, and the riverine culture developed along the Tagus, which flows from east to west into the Atlantic. The Spanish influence seems to diminish gradually towards the west. There are villages along the banks of the river, such as Vilafranca de Xira, that favour red skirts; but wealth is not displayed in the women's costumes. The cattle-breeders of the plains north of Lisbon wear knee breeches, usually dark blue or royal blue, red sashes, and either red or green waistcoats (colete), with a headbag of thick wool to match the waistcoat. The landowners, strangely enough, favour Andalucian riding costumes with short jackets and the broad-rimmed Cordobese hat.

It is remarkable that tradition has kept such a strong hold. In the northern third of Portugal, people consider Vigo (in Galician Spain) as the capital, and attention seems to concentrate on Vigo and not on Lisbon, the capital of Portugal. In the central part of Portugal, east of the Tagus, people look to Seville, and not to Lisbon. They take part in pilgrimages in and near Seville, as though that city was their capital.

The fisherfolk along the coasts of Portugal are said to be of a race all their own, coming originally from 'somewhere in the Near East'. This is borne out by the costume in the district of Aveiro, where the girls adorn their heads with a small round hat with two pompoms on the side, worn over a long black shawl. The dress of the fishergirls of Nazaré (named after Nazareth), some 90 miles north of Lisbon, has no parallel on the coasts of the Peninsula. Their speciality is some eleven underskirts of soft flannel, in various plain colours, and a check skirt over that, and the little round hat with two pompoms. An embroidered apron decorates the front of the skirt. The men wear much the same costume all along the coasts, except those of Povoa de Varzim, whose womenfolk knit them thick white woollen sweaters, bonnets and long socks, decorated with red and black cross-stitch designs, each knitter having her own special favourites. They are mostly traditional symbols, such as anchors, hearts, stylized trees, boats, fish, crescent moons, and the like. They are worn with plain black trousers.

Further south, in the hot districts of Beja and Evora, peasants will wear dull colours anyway. If they are cowboys tending cattle, they will have sheepskin aprons, slit down the middle for riding, with the wool on the outside, against the rain and cold blasts. Girls and women who work in the fields wear very broad-rimmed hats and long skirts pulled forward from the back, between their legs, then tucked into the stockings – which makes them appear to be wearing trousers. No doubt this fashion should be attributed to the practical necessity of avoiding insect bites and scratches from weeds.

This cursory glimpse of costume in Portugal may have given the reader a fuller picture of costume in the Iberian Peninsula.

EMBROIDERIES

Embroideries – like many other inventions in the life of a people – were invented for a purpose.

In the first place stitching was created to keep two pieces of leather or cloth together. To mend a part that was wearing away, extra stitching was added. Fancy stitching was evolved to make a repair more acceptable. Embroidery was seen to embellish material, and in the case of leather, it served the practical purpose of preventing the leather from wearing away so fast, or from showing dirt! Hence the fashion of embroidering soft leather, which is so prevalent in central Europe, Afghanistan, Czechoslovakia, parts of Russia and Andalucia (southern Spain). In Andalucia the cattle herders, who are in the saddle most of the day, wear leather aprons when they have to lasso steers or bulls. Otherwise, if the animal suddenly jerked away, in trying to escape from the lasso, the leather thongs of the lasso might cut into the thigh of the rider. These leather aprons are slit up the middle for easier riding. The designs on these aprons brighten and enrich the whole effect as well as preventing the aprons from looking dowdy or worn.

Embroidery, like lace, has evolved wherever life has become easier and people have had more time to spare from the labours of the soil, or tending animals. For example, the shepherds of the Landes in western France, who walk on stilts to watch their flocks in the lowlands near the sea, are expert knitters. They have time to knit many of their own garments, and in beween whiles they play their flutes – a well-known occupation among shepherds all over the world.

When women have finished their household duties and when not required to help in the fields, they have taken to lace-making and embroidering their clothes. The designs they have evolved bear a strong relationship to the beliefs of the people. For instance, from the time when sun-worship was prevalent, sunflower designs or six- and eight-pointed stars or 'rosettes' are preserved on sleeves, shawls, skirts or aprons. In central Europe and the Balkans, several districts have preserved the sunflower tradition in embroidery. In the Iberian Peninsula the most common symbols used in embroidery are: the heart, for love; the crescent moon, because the moon reigned over water, and rain was needed for the fields; it stood for the 'promise' of rain and therefore of good crops. The lozenge, a feminine symbol of creation since prehistoric times, is often seen; the wavy-line (curved or in zig-zag form) for water, or the so-called Greek pattern, also for water; it represents fertility. The olive branch means 'plenty', and is a favourite amongst Portuguese women and Spanish peasants living in the central and southern zones of the Peninsula. Peace and plenty are wanted everywhere. Vine leaves and grapes are a frequent design for similar reasons. The scallop shell is a luck symbol, meaning plenty, since shellfish was, and is, a staple food among those who live near the sea. It also means rebirth, water, fertility, while the spiral (from the shell of the snail) means creation or rebirth. A heart means love. A rose means woman, while a carnation means man.

In southern Spain there are also symbols imported from the Near East, at first by Phoenician traders and later by the Moors. One is the pomegranate, symbol of a family united and of 'fruitfulness', for it has many seeds. It was a sacred fruit in India, Egypt and Asia Minor. The tendrils of the vine mean love and affection. They are like arabesques, which came to Europe from the Near East, but are seen in embroideries here as well as in eastern countries. These tendrils are related to spirals, also symbols of creation or new life.

JEWELLERY AND COSTUME

Jewellery has been worn by men and women for many thousands of years. But it has not always been worn merely for embellishment. The Shamans of Siberia and Central Asia still wear what we might term jewellery for protective purposes. That is, they wear crescent moons, suns, and representations of planets made of iron, on their clothes, thus putting themselves under the protection of those heavenly bodies whose influence they invoke and believe in. It is their belief that, by wearing emblems of the sun, moon, etc, they are connected with the powers of these astral bodies, and that the shamans themselves will become more powerful, thanks to their help. Mircea Eliade in *Images and Symbols* tells us that some Siberian shamans' garments weigh up to thirty kilograms because of all their iron emblems, whose beneficent powers they wish to invoke.

As time passed, and with it the faith in these emblems, jewellery for adornment became the fashion. Yet still, even in cities, women and girls wear bracelets with 'charms'; tiny representations of the sun, moon, horn, heart, swastika, and so on for 'luck'. Some countries have charms against the 'evil eye', such as a circle within a lozenge, or a bead plainly decorated with an 'eye' as a protective amulet. The Near East, Asia and the Mediterranean countries are especially prolific in such charms.

In the Iberian Peninsula, brides and young children are especially protected against evil by having charms sewn on to their clothes. This occurs particularly in mountainous regions where older beliefs have persisted despite Christianity. Women may wear crescent-shaped earrings, popular in the whole of the northern half of the Peninsula. Exhaustive investigations have been carried out showing the evolution of the moon-face jewellery to the plain crescent-shaped earrings and pendants. The Folk Museum in Madrid has a fine collection of such jewellery. A horn (whether made of horn, coral, jet or ferrous metal) is another frequently seen amulet worn for luck, for it is essentially a phallus, emblem of fertility, bringing plenty. Belief in the potency of the horns of bulls, cows and deer derives from the time when these animals were worshipped as deities because they were the source of food. A fig is also favoured as bringer of 'plenty' because it contains many seeds. The early Greeks worshipped the god Priapus, whose emblem was a fig, but whose origin is lost in the mists of time (it is no accident that Adam and Eve are described as wearing fig leaves, the emblem of fructification, as mentioned in the Bible story). All these emblems were – and still are – in use in some regions of the Peninsula; fashioned in durable material like jet, coral, metals, precious and semi-precious stones, they were worn on, or sewn on to, bridal costumes and infants' clothes.

Pearls and shells are, or were, a universal symbol of fertility, plenty, good luck, re-birth in the afterlife, water and riches. Mircea Eliade explains their importance to early man, and from then throughout his development to present times. Among western European cultures, shells are still used as decorative motifs in jewellery and architecture.

Pearls and oyster shells have been found in the graves of prehistoric man, in Egyptian tombs, in burials in several European countries and in parts of Africa and Asia. Cowrie shells are used as money among some African tribes, and some use them as necklaces, for luck.

Pearls were considered by early man as the offspring of the shell, therefore they promoted fertility or new life. It is not for nothing that Aphrodite was the Greek goddess of love, for she represented the pearl.

Pearls are rarely seen in the Peninsula as regional jewellery. Only in Valencia and the city of Salamanca do pearls belong to the costume. This may be due to their rarity, but it is possible that they were brought to Valencia and Salamanca in special circumstances. Historically the Greeks considered Aphrodite (and the Romans Venus) as a pearl emerging from the sea, the fruit of the sea, the child of the sea – that primordial element from whence all creation emerged. For a pearl is an emblem of creation, and it may have been brought to Valencia by Greek traders. Yet other well-known Greek trading colonies like Ampurias, as well as those further south, in Andalucia, do not sport pearls on their costumes. As for Salamanca, it is a mystery. It is also a mystery how Salamanca has been a centre for the manufacture of fine jewellery, just like that worked in Ephesus. For instance, in both regions, brooches, earrings, buttons, in gold and silver filigree, are shaped like breasts with a nipple. These were obviously designed to put the wearer under the protection of Artemis the Earth Mother, worshipped in ancient Ephesus.

Sequins

It has been acknowledged that sequins are an imitation of fish scales. By wearing fish scales, the wearer could be identified with the fish, an emblem of fertility. Some modern dresses are covered with sequins which make the wearer look like a sleek fish, shiny and slippery, and very attractive. No wonder that early man was seduced by the idea of wearing fish scales, since it brought him (so it was thought) 'plenty'. He had noticed that fish lay countless eggs, therefore to wear fish scales would bring women a large family.

Mother-of-pearl discs on women's clothes, as seen in parts of India, are another symbol of luck. Sea shells contain a source of food, therefore shells are lucky. By wearing the lining of the shell (mother-of-pearl), women believed they would be lucky in child-bearing. The discs are kept in place by fancy stitching round the disc, and the general effect is most attractive.

To protect humans from evil influences, amulets and emblems were sewn on to garments, but we must not forget the horses and mules, who must also be protected from evils. They were depended upon for millenia as reliable transport in European and Asian countries, and were therefore of primary importance. This can certainly be ascertained along the Levantine coast of Spain, where animals are bedecked with heavy cloth trappings of immense size and an unbelievable number of fancy tassels, some reaching the ground, and all covered with appliqué designs embellished with countless tiny globe mirrors and mother-of-pearl discs, all worked in fancy stitching, creating a multi-coloured vision of splendour and richness, glittering in the sunshine.

Coloured glass discs and mirrors are also used for luck and as a protection among male ritual dancers in the Peninsula, as well as all over the southern parts of Europe. In some districts such as Avila and Extremadura (central Meseta and the West), women's hats also carry these prophylactic mirrors to ward off evils like sterility, disease, and the evil eye. Some little shells, like buttons, are worn to bring the wearer money. The French Mascarade dancers *Les Beaux* also wear pearls and sequins on their wonderful garments and the 'horse' wears mirrors on his head-dress, which makes him quite resplendent! In parts of the Near and Middle East, men as well as women wear on their clothes, round their neck, in their ears, or on the horse's trappings, a glass or ceramic eye, to avoid the evil eye. I have known mothers who sewed such eyes to the bindings of their son's jackets when he went abroad to study. The eyes are usually blue and some emblems have three eyeballs fixed back to back, so wherever you look, one eye always deflects the evil away.

COLOURS

Each colour has its own significance. Red is the colour of life and love, therefore red flannel petticoats are worn in most parts of the Peninsula, except near the Mediterranean coast, where it is far too hot. Green is the emblem of the regeneration of nature, or spring, meaning new life. Blue is for purity and the bright sky, meaning good weather and ripening of crops. Yellow and orange are the colours of the sun and of wisdom. White is for purity and innocence. Purple and black are the colours of mourning, therefore they are *not* included in the rituals of sympathetic magic. The 'good' colours are worn by most teams of ritual men dancers all over European countries. In some cases they just wear ribbons hanging from the neck-line, or from the crown of the hat or the brim at the back, or even on the jackets, attached like tabs. Sometimes the ribbons are fixed to one end of the dancing sticks, used in dances like our Morris dances.

We have seen that black was related to the underworld, the land of the spirits, of regeneration of nature, the land of the womb of the Earth Mother, where she 'matures' ores, metals and crystals and from where the dead are reborn into either 'another world' (paradise or hell, according to their merits while alive) or reincarnated and given another chance to live out a better life here once more. The Indian belief in reincarnation according to merits in this life is well-known.

Black is the colour of mourning in the western world (although white is the colour of mourning in India). In the Iberian Peninsula, black is worn by widows for the rest of their lives, but other relatives wear black for three to five years according to the closeness of their relationship to the dead person. Purple is worn for some time, then comes freedom to wear what you will. It is all regulated according to their relationship with the dead. However, black is worn by all during Holy Week in Andalucia, for the mourning is for Christ. Black lace mantillas are worn by the women, married or not. After Holy Week the girls launch out into lovely pale or bright colours and once more become birds of paradise or better still flowers! Widows, of course, remain in black.

A girl of marriageable age should look attractive, so for feast days in Andalucia, she wears a bright or pale frilly dress, a high comb and white lace mantilla. But in the rest of Spain local regional costumes are worn for feast days, and not high combs and lace mantillas, except in Valencia, where a special comb only is worn. This one is made of metal, as opposed to the Andalucian comb which is of tortoiseshell (nowadays, plastic). In all parts of Spain a red carnation is worn or carried in the hand, for a carnation means a man, and by wearing one the girl announces her readiness to get married. In Cataluña white lace mantillas are worn in some villages for feast days, but not a comb.

The only exception I know of about wearing black when not in mourning, is in Braga (Portugal) where black is worn by brides, the dress being covered in jet and black sequins and small beads, for black is a respectable colour, and a bride must no longer attract the attention of any man except her husband. In Cataluña a bride will sometimes wear black for the same reason, although later she may wear other colours if living in a town, where customs are often relaxed. Another country where married women will usually wear black is Italy, again because black is a respectable colour.

In spite of the traditional significance of colours, stage choreographers pay no attention to local beliefs. They will dress their dancers in violet, black or mauve colours and think themselves clever for showing something unusual. They seem to have no notion of tradition. For example, foreigners may go to Spain, learn some dances, then form a group of their own under an assumed Spanish name (not their own name) and they and their group wear any colours, black or purple included, regardless. And when they go abroad and form a group outside Spain, they will make up steps and figures that have nothing to do with dances of the country they claim to represent. They seem to have no conscience about breaking traditions or pretending to perform regional dances when they themselves have distorted dance and customs. I know several people who do that, and have no compunction in inventing movements in dances, thereby rendering those dances meaningless. They have succeeded in making the dances physical exercises to music and not folk dances any longer.

CHAPTER SIX

Castanets and musical instruments in the Iberian Peninsula

As mentioned earlier, early man had a constant aim and that was to find enough food for himself and his family. He gathered wild fruits, hunted wild animals and birds, collected shellfish and snails and the seeds of wild plants, and he fished. After many thousands of years he learned to cultivate grain. He saw that some seashells had a pearl between the two lobes, and he came to believe that these pearls were the 'new life' or offspring of the shell. So the women pinned pearls onto their clothes to ensure their own fertility. In order to hear the voice of the shells the two lobes were strung together at their base and clicked to make a sound calling the spirit of the shell to come and create a further supply of shellfish. In some parts of western Spain such as Galicia, these shells are still used in folk dances to beat out the rhythm. They are held by a string to the thumb, over the knuckle, the round part hanging down. Some people put the string over the middle fingers, flick the wrists back and forth to mark the rhythm, and thus attract the spirit of the shells and ask for fertility. These shells are also used in the dance by rubbing their backs together to make a grinding noise. Shells are the original castanets.

It was all right for people living near the sea, but people living inland also wanted fertility, so they carved imitation shells in wood. The wood they chose was the chestnut tree because it had numerous fruit and was therefore a fertility symbol, so it was the best material to ensure continuity. It was called '*castaña*', hence the name '*castañeta*' or '*castañuela*'.

In Andalucia the string is held on the thumb, on either side of the knuckle, where the thumb fits the curve of the hand. The left-hand castanet is 'male' and it marks the rhythm of the dance. The right-hand castanet is 'female' and is half a tone higher than the male. The left hand keeps the basic rhythm, beating on beats. The fingers of the right hand are moved quickly across the belly of the castanet, striking it with the four fingers one after the other starting with the little finger, before the left-hand castanet strikes the beat. So one counts 1, 2, 3, 4 and 5 (the left hand), according to the timing of the music. For a special step in starting or ending, both castanets are sounded together, which makes a louder noise.

The use of castanets must be very ancient because a pair of ivory castanets were found in a coffin in ancient Egypt, dating from long before the birth of Christ.

Nowadays castanets are used equally by men and women in the dance, but only in Andalucia are they played as described above. Everywhere else in the country they are worn on the two middle fingers. The palms are held uppermost and away from the body and the instruments beaten against the palms, by both hands simultaneously. In Andalucia, the palms are held sideways or downwards so that the fingers can beat the lobes of the castanets against each other. In many parts of Spain ribbons are attached to the castanets, but not in Andalucia.

In Andalucia castanets can be used while the arms move right round making a circle, each arm alternately, whereas if the castanets are strung on the middle fingers and the wrists jerk to mark time, then the arms are held up, above the head and a little forward, to imitate the horns of the sacred bull god, and/or the crescent moon – deity of the night.

Castanets are used in most dances in the Peninsula, but not in all flamenco dances, because the 'snake' arm and finger movements must be represented. At times fingers are snapped, or in the extreme south 'chinchines' are used. These are tiny finger cymbals, as used in Persia and in some parts of Turkey. Clapping of the hands helps the rhythm, and also indicates the transition from one part of the dance to the next, when the musician has to be warned.

Percussion instruments in the form of two small sticks were, and still are, used in Persia and in the Middle and Near East by dancers, presumably to accentuate the rhythm, as is still done in northern Portugal. There they are called 'chulas'.

In Galicia and Asturias, the north-west of Spain, the gaita (bagpipes) are the favourites. They are also called *gaita de foles* (wind pipes). A drum usually accompanies this instrument.

Further east, in Cantabria and towards the Basque country, a pipe (not bagpipes) and drum, often played by the same man, supply the accompaniment to song and dance. In the Basque country itself, a pipe called '*txistu*' at times played with both hands, and a drum, are the norm. In the mountainous parts of the Basque country, a special very long drum of ancient design is still found. It is shaped like an elongated bull's head (now very modified), and has four strings which are struck with a stick making a dull sound. This is called a *ttun-ttun*.

In central Spain a shawm player and a drummer are the usual accompanists, the shawm being called a *gaita* (like the bagpipes); is some parts it is called a *dulzaina*. In some districts a guitar will accompany them, but this is unusual.

In Aragón, the north-east, guitarists, often with a drummer too, play for the jotas and other dances.

Along the eastern coast of Spain, in Cataluña, bands called *coblas* play for the local sardanas and other local folk dances. The coblas consist of eleven instruments, all wind, except for a cello and a drum. The leader has a tiny drum strapped to his wrist, and he plays the introductory notes on his flageolet. The cello is, of course, a modern addition.

If we go westwards from Cataluña into the province of Valencia, we find pipe and drum and guitars, at times mixed, sometimes separately played, and occasionally each type of instrument accompanies a different part of a dance.

The province of Murcia, further west, has chiefly guitars, and in Andalucia, guitars have taken over completely; not surprising, since this type of instrument was first introduced into Europe by the Moors in 711 AD and spread from there into most of Europe.

The *pandereta* (tambourine) is played all over the Peninsula. In the northern regions it is played mainly by women, for it originally represented the full moon, and was therefore representative of women, but men also play it. In many regions streamers of various bright colours hang from its sides, so that – as in Valencian regions – when fertility dances with high kicks and twirls are performed, the tambourine is shaken so that the ribbons look like rain. In the region of Málaga huge tambourines are played by a finger being scraped along the skin, very rapidly, thus making a sound similar to drumming. This enormous type of tambourine is said to have come from Morocco. In the central western regions of Spain and parts of Portugal a square tambourine called a *pandero* is used.

In all parts of Spain castanets are played, except in Cataluña; the Greek influence there produced a bird-like movement of the hands, with the middle finger bent inwards, the others stretched out, the wrists bent down, the elbows and arms shoulder high, the arms always curved. They are moved from left to right and back again, jerking the wrists round to mark time. The aim of this flicking is to make the hands represent the dove, bird of the Earth Mother Goddess or Aphrodite. Arms held in a crescent-moon shape are usual in the rest of Spain.

In the southern half of Portugal guitars are played, but further north the pipe and drum are more usual.

In the Braga region, men wear tiny castanets about one-and-a-half inches long, fixed on the thumb; otherwise I have never seen any castanets in that country (except for stage imitation flamenco). Bagpipes are found in the extreme north, the Minho district, dating back to when Portugal was still part of Spain.

Bibliography

Alford, Violet, *The Traditional Dance* (Methuen) London, 1935 [with Gallop, R.]

— *Pyrenean Festivals* (Chatto & Windus) London, 1937

— *Introduction to English Folklore* (G. Bell & Co.) London, 1952

— *The Singing of the Travels* (Max Parrish) London, 1956

— *Sword Dance and Drama* (Merlin Press) London, 1962

Baroja, Julio Caro, *Los Pueblos de España* (Barna) Barcelona, 1946

— *Revista de Dialectologia y Tradiciones Populares* Madrid, 1965

Bates, Oric, *The Eastern Lybians* (Library of African Studies) 1970

Blanchard, R., *Le Bac'cubert: A Book of Healing Dances* Paris, 1914

Bowra, Sir Cecil Maurice, *The Heritage of Symbolism* (Macmillan & Co.) London, 1951

— *Primitive Song* (Weidenfeld & Nicolson) London, 1962

Budge, Sir E. A. Wallis, *From Fetish to God in Ancient Egypt* (Arno Press) New York, 1977

Cirilli, René, *Les Prêtres Danseurs de Rome* Paris, 1958

Conrad, Jack Randolph, *The Horn and the Sword* (McGibbon & Kee) New York, 1959

Cook, A. B., *Zeus: A Study in Ancient Religion* (Cambridge University Press) Cambridge, 1925

D'Albert, C., *Encyclopaedia of Dancing* (T. M. Middleton) London, 1920

D'Alviella, Count Goblet, *The Migration of Symbols* (Aquarian Pub. Co.) London, 1979

Del Arco, Ricardo, *Costumbres y Trajes en los Pirineos* Zaragoza, 1930

— *Aragón* Huesca, 1931

Del Rio, J., *Danzas Tipicas Burgalesas* Burgos, 1959
Driberg, J. N., *The People of the Small Arrow* (Harcourt, Brack Co.) New York, 1939
Echagüe, José Ortiz, *España: Tipos y Trajes* (Publicaciones Ortiz Echagüe) Bilbao, 1953
Eliade, Mircea, *Myths, Dreams and Mysteries* (Harvill Press) London, 1960
— *Images and Symbols* (Harvill Press) London, 1961
— *The Forge and the Crucible* (Rider & Co.) London, 1962
— *Shamanism* (Routledge & Kegan Paul) London, 1964
— *Méphistophélès et l'Androgyne* and five other books in French
Elworthy, F. T., *Horns of Honour* (J. Murray) London, 1900
Epton, Nina, *Spanish Fiestas* (Cassell) London, 1968
Farbridge, Maurice H., *Studies in Biblical and Semitic Symbolism* (Kegan Paul, Trench, Trubner) London, 1923
Farrés, Aurelio Capmany, *El Ball y la Danza a Cataluña* Barcelona, 1948
Frankfurt, Henri, *Kingship and the Gods* (University of Chicago Press) Chicago, 1978
Frazer, James G., *The Golden Bough* (Macmillan & Co.) London, 1933
Gallop, Rodney, *A Book of the Basques* (University of Nebraska Press) Lincoln USA, 1981 [see also Alford, V.]
Gennep, Arnold Van, *The Rites of Passage* (Routledge & Kegan Paul) London, 1977
Harrison, Jane Ellen, *Themis* (Merlin Press) London, 1977
— *Prologomena to the Study of Greek Religion* (Merlin Press) London, 1980
Hawkes, Jacquetta, *The Dawn of the Gods* (Sphere Books) London, 1972
Hughes, Pennethorne, *Witchcraft* (Longman) London, 1952
James, Edwin Oliver, *Prehistoric Religion* (Thames & Hudson) London, 1957
— *The Cult of the Mother Goddess* (Thames & Hudson) London, 1959

JASTROW, Morris, *The Religion of Babylon and Assyria* (Ginn & Co.) Boston USA, 1898

JEANMAIRE, Henri, *Couroi et Courètes* (Université de Lille) Lille, 1939

JUNG, Carl Gustav, *Collected Works in English* (Routledge & Kegan Paul) London, 1978

LAWLER, Lilian Beatrice, *The Dance in Ancient Greece* (A. & C. Black) London, 1964

LEACH, Edmund Ronald, *Lecture to the Royal Anthropological Institute* London, 1968

LEVY, Gertrude, *The Gate of Horn* (Faber & Faber) London, 1964

MARRINGER, J., *The Code of Prehistoric Man* (Weidenfeld & Nicolson) London, 1956

MEEK, Theophile J., *Hebrew Origins* (Hamish Hamilton) London, 1950

MOURGUES, Marcelle, *La Danse Provençale* Cannes, 1956

PEREZ, P. Constante Pablo, *Notas Viejas Calicianas* Vigo, 1925

POWELL, T. G. E., *The Celts* (Thames & Hudson) London, 1983

PROVENCE, M., *Symbolisme des Danses Provençales.*

SACHS, Curt, *World History of the Dance* (W. W. Norton) New York, 1963

SAILLENS, E., *Nos Vierges Noires* (Éditions Universelles) Paris, 1945

SPENCE, Lewis, *Myth and Ritual in Dance, Game and Rhyme* (Watts & Co.) London, 1942

— *The Mysteries of Britain* (Aquarian Press) Wellingborough, 1970

STARKIE, Walter, *Musician's Journey Through Spain* Geneva, 1958

TROUBET, J., *Les Danses du Chevalet* 1975